Grace For The Grieving

Grace for the Grieving

A Compilation from a Grief Group

Authors / Contributors

Jeannine Richardson
Bob Warnke
Maureen Revak
John Kidder
Harriet Perry
Burt and Jill Groenheim
Karen Huebschman

Grace for the Grieving: A Compilation from a Grief Group
Copyright © 2018 by Haven on Rice Creek, LLC.

Third Edition, 2025

ALL RIGHTS RESERVED. No part of this book may be reproduced or utilized in any form or by any means, electronic or mechanical including photocopying, recording, or by any information storage and retrieval system, except in the case of brief quotations embodied in critical articles and reviews, without permission in writing from the publisher.

The authors / organization have made every effort to ensure that the accuracy of the information within this book was correct at the time of publication. The author does not assume and hereby disclaims any liability to any party for any loss, damage, or disruption caused by errors or omissions, whether such errors or omissions result from accident, negligence, or any other cause.

Unless otherwise indicated All Scripture references are from the Holy Bible, New International Version®, NIV® Copyright ©1973, 1978, 1984, 2011 by Biblica, Inc.® Used by permission. All rights reserved worldwide.

Scripture references marked ESV are from the ESV® Bible (The Holy Bible, English Standard Version®) copyright © 2001 by Crossway Bibles, a publishing ministry of Good News Publishers. The ESV® text has been reproduced in cooperation with and by permission of Good News Publishers. Unauthorized reproduction of this publication is prohibited. All rights reserved.

ISBN: 979-8-9927795-0-9

Photography and Interior design by Jeannine Richardson and Bob Warnke.

For information and inquiries, please contact Haven on Rice Creek, LLC.
www.havenonricecreek.org.

For information on purchasing additional copies or on facilitating a group in your area, please contact havenonricecreek@gmail.com.

Printed in the United States of America

Grace for the Grieving is a work of love. It is truly a gentle, caring support in a time of deep and unfathomable pain for all of us to find comfort. We grieve in so many ways throughout our lives that I think this book can bring comfort to people who are experiencing any deep loss in their lives. God's presence comes alive through the support of our "fellow" travelers. Thank you to each of the contributors for taking the time to write and share this magnificent journey. I especially love the photographs. I think that when words fail, as they often do, a vision of peace can heal many wounds. I will cherish these words and visual inspirations as I, friends, and loved ones move through life's loves and losses.

~Mary O'Shaughnessy, Psy.D., N.P.P.
Silent Presence: A Companion Through the Journey of Grief

Grace for the Grieving is nothing short of being "heart touching" and "heart healing." The testimonies given, minister to the souls of those who are dealing with the sudden loss of a loved one, guiding them through the grieving process. It picks up after the initial loss, the funeral service, and the time that was spent ministering to their heart. I am very grateful to have such a beneficial book in my local church to give.

~Wayne Colonna, Lead Pastor
South Florida Bible Fellowship

Table of Contents

Introduction	1
One - Experiencing Grief	41
Two - Extending Grace	53
Three - The Struggle with Faith	65
Four - Secondary Losses	79
Five - Forgiveness	91
Six - Finding Hope	101
Seven - Identity after Loss	109
Eight - Keeping the Memory Alive	119
Additional Stories of Loss	129
References / Resources	142
Books to Build and Restore	143
Bible References	148
Verses by Topic	149
Definitions	151
Unhealthy Myths and Erroneous Beliefs of Grieving	153
Notes	155
Journaling	156
My Story	158
A Closing Note	160
About the Contributors...	161

Acknowledgment

*A Special Thanks to Russ Falstad, our facilitator.
He faithfully and patiently guided our group through the
tearful journey of grief and gave constant encouragement
in the writing of this study guide.*

*We would also like to thank everyone who contributed
to the process of making this book possible.*

*To those of you who walk alongside the grieving and
brokenhearted, we offer our sincere
and heartfelt appreciation.
Your presence and prayers are more
valuable than you will ever know.*

Praise to the God of All Comfort:

2 Corinthians 1:3–4

*Praise be to the God and Father of our Lord Jesus Christ,
the Father of compassion and the God of all comfort,
who comforts us in all our troubles, so
that we can comfort those in any
trouble with the comfort we ourselves receive from God.*

The Defining Moments of Our Lives ...

We all have them, and we all need them. They influence who we are and how we view ourselves in this incredible journey called life.

Some moments we forget, as they were only important in the context of the season we were in during that time of our life. Other moments burn with embarrassment, feeling naked and exposed, we don't like what we see or the possibility that others would see us in that way.

Eventually, we dismiss those memories leaving only awkward fragments behind. Then there are the moments that change our lives forever...death, when time stands still. You become an outsider...watching your life in disbelief.

Nightmare, with eyes wide open.
Unable to comprehend.
Shock sets in.
Grief takes over.

Our lives ... like the seasons, collective moments in time.

Springtime...when hope stirs, life feels fresh and clean. Buds turn to blossoms, vivid colors, gentle fragrance, soft nourishing rain...hope springs forth and all things seem possible.

Summer...the days are long, and life is full. You accomplish much in the warmth of the sun and easily find rest from the heat of day with the simplicity that comes from a cool glass of water. Life seems peaceful in summertime.

Autumn...arrives with a smokescreen of conflict, relief and sadness wrapped in hues of gold, orange, red, and brown, softly landing on barren ground. We huddle around campfires with feeble attempts to warm the chilled air. Flames burn bright with reflection of all that we have left undone...time wasted on temporal things. Flames lower and smolder as fall turns to ash.

Winter...quiet, cold, lonely, bitter winds blow deep into the frozen tundra of the soul. Sunlight sparkles dancing on snow drifts...teasing of warmth...betrayed by reality. The sting of frost penetrates the flesh...deep into bone and blood runs cold...deeper into memories and emotions run cold. Long sleepless nights losing yourself in the shadows of what once was.

Such is grief.
Such are the seasons of grief...

We cannot stop these seasons. Just as spring gives way to summer, and summer to fall, and fall to winter. Springtime will come again with all her finery, fragrance and promise of life.

Hope awakens, and we will live...again.

~Jeannine

"Every man's life ends the same way; it is only the details of how he lived and how he died that distinguish one man from another."

~Ernest Hemingway

Introduction

The personal stories you will read in this grief manual are those of regular people from rural Wisconsin who have all experienced the loss of either a spouse, child, parent or other family member. We came together as part of a grief group at one of the local churches. We started out by sharing our stories. As heart-wrenching as it is to relive a loved one's death, there is healing in telling our stories, yet some people were too overcome to share that first night. Compassion stirred as we listened, cried, and comforted one another. We continued meeting weekly, working our way through a faith-based grief curriculum, and we soon recognized that sharing not only our grief but also our Christian faith was the foundation for our healing. These became the common threads that wove us together.

We felt so blessed to have found each other and wanted others to have that same experience. We discussed facilitating other grief groups but found out the material we used was out of print. Out of a need to pay it forward (and maybe a desire to keep meeting on a regular basis), we discussed writing our own material. We felt our healing wasn't so much based on the material we read but the discussions that

INTRODUCTION

occurred each week. Sometimes we stayed on topic with the material—other times we went completely off course. The camaraderie we developed was so powerful and healing, we knew we needed to give others the opportunity to find comfort in their own grief group.

So, we set out to write a grief manual. We are not professional grief counselors, psychologists, or writers. We consist of a farmer, a recruiter, an accountant, a banker, a health care provider, a veteran, an automotive technician, and homemakers. We are presenting this material in hopes of support and healing for those that are grieving. We do not pretend to have the knowledge of theology to explain the reasoning of God, nor define portions of scripture. The material references biblical and humanist sources for further study. Theological questioning should be addressed to your church pastor or Christian counselor. If you are concerned that grief has turned to depression, we would encourage you or someone you care for to seek professional counsel.

This study guide does not have all the answers. It is simply meant to spur discussion. Because faith has been such an important part of our healing, it is woven in throughout these pages. It is not our intention to preach but simply to explain how God and faith helped us through our journey.

We feel it is important that we tell our stories of loss so that you can relate to us and know that as you journey through this season of grief, or if you are supporting someone who is grieving, you are not alone and there is ... *grace for the grieving*.

May you find comfort and peace in the journey.

Jeannine's Story

I met Londe in August of 1977. I had seen him a few times around the shipyard where we both worked on Trident submarines as welders. This particular day was different. I sat at the top of the unfinished missile room, sitting on an upside down 5-gallon bucket. I looked over my job order for the evening and chatted with the crew leader. I heard footsteps as they approached, pounding against the heavy metal scaffolding, coming closer and closer before stopping. I moved my eyes slowly from my welding gear that I gathered in front of me to the work boots that were now just a few feet away. I can still remember as my eyes slowly took in the scene. He wore steel-toe work boots, not the standard issue; these were a richly polished brown, well-worn, but clean. Straight leg jeans rested at the ankle; no one wore straight legs anymore and these looked good; they were clean—no rips or burns—just a relaxed fit and easy on the eyes. His flannel shirt was untucked; the sleeves were rolled up just enough to expose the thick veins in his strong forearms. He had his gear slung over his left shoulder, his hard hat was on backward, and he wore no safety glasses (a blatant violation of OSHA standards). He had style. He set himself apart from the thousands of dirty coverall-clad coworkers that I shared 2nd shift with. Yes, even at work in a shipyard, he definitely had style. As I took it all in, it was his eyes that drew me. The sun was setting behind me and it cast the most amazing golden glow upon him. Our eyes met and, in that moment, that one breathless moment in time, we connected. No words were exchanged, but none were needed. The stage was set for what would become a beautiful backdrop to our marriage and the next 34 years of our life together.

INTRODUCTION

Two years later we moved to northwestern Wisconsin. Coming from Connecticut to this small Midwestern town of about 2000 people was like stepping back 20 years in time. It was a delightful change to the fast pace we were accustomed to, but it was not welcoming for an interracial couple in 1979. Many times, I wanted to just give up and go back home. Racism was alive and well. The stares of disgust and the whispers that surrounded us took me by surprise. I was unprepared when no one would rent to us or employ us. I was unprepared for the life-threatening phone calls we received to try and run us out of town. Londe would not give in; he would not give up. He would not be run from the town that he vacationed in as a child—a town where he dreamed of living and raising his family. He determined that we would be trailblazers, we would do this together, and we would do this with God. I felt safe with him as he promised with God's help to protect me, to protect us, and to protect the family we had not yet begun. Even though I believed that I was born for this challenge, my spirit felt crushed as I began to understand firsthand the sting of racism, the sting of being hated, and the sting of having to look over my shoulder in fear. We clung to each other, we clung to God, and that served to make us stronger.

How does one prepare for the crushing blows of life? I couldn't... I could not prepare anymore for that season of life than I could prepare for his long illness and his death that would come 32 years later.

Faith gets tested, and through the years ours was tested often. Londe would always manage to center me back in Christ when the hard things of life seemed to press in on all sides: finances, raising kids, friendships betrayed, illness, etc. He would pull me into his arms and whisper softly and confidently, "it's gonna be okay, you're gonna be okay, we're gonna be okay." With his arms around me, I felt safe. I was not alone in this world; we were together, we faced things together, and we faced things with God.

The next 25 years overflowed with family life; raising six kids, play dates, birthday parties, school years, sporting events, teenage rebellion, college tours, and the arrival of grandchildren. Life was full, life was good, and life was exhausting.

By June 2006, my once-patient, tower-of-strength husband that I had always known and relied on was becoming more distant from me. He was so tired all the time, which made him irritable and discouraged. I had made numerous doctors' appointments for him, and he would "forget" to go. At my wits' end, I eventually made one more appointment and told him he needed to get this figured out and find out if there was something wrong, because we could not go on like this anymore.

I remember coming out of the grocery store on a Friday afternoon; it was raining hard. I started the car and turned on the wipers when my cell phone rang. It was Londe. "Jeans, I went to the doctor. It's not good."

I froze. My heart began to pound so hard I could barely hear myself ask him, "What do you mean? What did he say?"

He remained silent for what seemed to be an eternity before he calmly stated, "It looks like I may have leukemia ... I need to go for more testing in Duluth on Monday." I couldn't speak. I couldn't process the words he had just spoken. It didn't make

INTRODUCTION

sense—nothing about those words made sense. He said it as if he were telling me he had to work late. In that moment, I could only hear the thumping of the windshield wipers as they raced back and forth and the sound of my heart racing even faster ... only everything moved in slow motion. "Are you there?" he whispered.

"Yes," I said, choking back the tears. But the truth was I didn't know where I was ... confusion overwhelmed me. My mind raced as my life stopped in that frightening moment. I thought to myself, "No, this is something that happens to other people, not to us. Leukemia? What does this mean? There must have been a mistake." I told him I would be right home, but I sat in the parking lot, unable to move, just staring at my phone and listening to the wipers. I couldn't see anything, and I couldn't remember how to drive. I could not function and so I sat there, and I cried. I took a deep breath; I hated this moment with every fiber of my being. Fear consumed me ... I had never felt so scared in all my life.

Somehow, I made my way home, and we held each other, and he whispered, "It's gonna be okay, I'm gonna be okay, we're gonna be okay." I wanted to believe him. I needed to believe him.

He moved through treatment like everything else he had ever done—with strength and bravery. He never complained. We drew close and he drew closer to God. Over the next five years we were keenly aware that this was a gift, that his life and our life together was a gift that would eventually come to an end. On August 30th, 2011, the doctor shared with us that there was nothing more they could do. We sat there in disbelief as the doctor said, "Best case scenario, you may have a year, but most likely 3–6 months." How are you supposed to process something like that? I couldn't breathe. We just sat there searching each other's eyes. I wished that we would somehow wake up from this bad dream and life would be good again, back on course with all the hopes and dreams that we shared for a future of growing old together, but there were no words. We were both in too much pain to talk about it. Telling the kids became yet another painful process. The fear and pain that they each carried felt like more than I could bear.

One night as we lay in bed, he took my hand and rested it on his chest. I could feel his heart pounding. He thanked me for being there, for loving him, and for all the years that we shared together. Warm tears quietly wet the pillow as I tried so very hard to be brave. I didn't want him to know I was crying because I didn't want to add to his pain by causing him to worry about me. He began to pray. I listened to the most unselfish prayer that I had ever heard, as he quietly and earnestly asked the Lord to take care of our family, to take care of me, and to please not let his death turn any of our children away from Him but instead to draw them each closer to God. I don't know if I slept that night or any of the remaining nights over the next three weeks as we watched him grow weaker and weaker, day after day. The strong arms and body that once held and protected me were becoming thin and frail before my eyes. As we all gathered around him that final weekend at Mayo clinic, we talked to him, we played music for him, and we prayed over him. When he finally took his last breath, he opened his eyes and tracked until he caught my gaze and, in that moment, that final moment, we connected one last time. He tried to speak but only mouthed the words "Love ... you ..." and I watched as life left his eyes.

INTRODUCTION

The days that followed were blurry. Our children each stepped up, came alongside me, and alongside each other as funeral plans had to be made. We pushed past the pain that filled us all. The funeral director told me later that there were over 600 people that attended the visitation and funeral. I had no clue; I only knew the line remained steady for hours as friends and neighbors gathered and wept. When it became quiet and all had left the visitation, I held his hand one last time, kissed his forehead and whispered, "You done good, darlin'. Thirty-two years ago, they wanted to run you out of town, and now they cry and don't want to see you go. It was no easy run, but it was a good run—so proud of you." The next day our six children chose to be his pallbearers. They all agreed that their dad had always carried them, so it was their honor to carry him. It was another moment in time that will remain with me forever.

I have come to understand that we must endure and learn how to grow through every season of life, whether good or bad. There are no rehearsals in this life. We must simply do our best to live and share God's love. And that was what Londe and I did. Over the years people blessed us with opportunities. We never took that for granted and in turn we did our best to be thriving members of our community. We raised six loving children, and we shared our lives, our home, and our faith with others.

Londe Richardson

Londe was born June 26, 1953, in New London, Connecticut, and was raised in Mystic, CT, with his three younger siblings. His mother was a nurse and his father a state trooper. At the age of 11, his mother was badly burned in a fire and was hospitalized for many months. During this time, he took on the task of helping his father to care for his younger siblings. This difficult experience eventually served him well in developing the responsibility and compassion that would shape him into a loving and nurturing father to his own six children.

Londe and I married on March 16, 1981. He lived as a faithful husband, father, and man of God with a heart of compassion for others. During difficult times he always put into perspective how blessed we were (as there were always others less fortunate) and how we needed to be grateful for what God had provided. His positive outlook and prayers for others continued even during the most taxing times of his illness. As a natural and passionate athlete, Londe played basketball, baseball, and wallyball in many of the community men's leagues. He graciously stepped back from playing to allow his children, as he put it, "their turn to shine." He coached their youth leagues so he could be involved with them, as he prioritized family time. He attended every game he could and when his illness kept him housebound, he would listen to their games that were broadcast on the radio so he could discuss and coach them when they returned home.

INTRODUCTION

A hard-working route salesman and machinist, Londe labored long hours and often picked up second jobs to make ends meet. He never complained. People knew him as a steady, even-tempered man who could always be counted on to follow through on his word. He despised gossip and dishonesty and believed in helping others whenever possible. Throughout his life he endured the sting of racism, and I watched him repeatedly and calmly choose the high road. He was the strongest person I had ever known, only allowing adversity to change him for the better. He loved being a husband, a father, and a grandfather. He was proud of his family. The character and kindness toward others that each of his children displayed was most important to him. Londe possessed humility along with a good sense of humor. When people commented on his handsome family, he playfully told them, "The kids get their good looks from their mom ... I only added a touch of color."

Surrounded by family, Londe went home to be with the Lord on September 19, 2011.

Bob's Story

Spooner Wesleyan Church announced they were organizing a Nicaraguan mission crew for the end of January 2016. My wife Brenda had talked about going in previous years, but the timing had not worked. This year she was led to go, and I joined in her enthusiasm without hesitation. In the weeks prior to leaving, we shopped together for school supplies, backpacks, face paint, and trinkets for the kids. We joined our group at the airport and left with the anticipation of construction work at a school (San Juan La Plywood), playing with the children, and helping families.

We started at the work site on Monday. Our first job was removing dirt from an area using shovels and buckets. It was a hot, breezy day in the mid-90s, and the dust became so thick and dank that we eventually pulled our bandanas up and breathed through them. By the end of the first day, our nostrils were black, and we were tired.

On Tuesday and Wednesday, the ladies stayed in Managua and prepared backpacks and school supplies for the children. On Wednesday, they distributed those supplies, and Brenda met the children and parents. On the days that the ladies were in Managua, the men traveled to and from the work site. On Thursday and Friday, Brenda rejoined us at the construction site. She and another volunteer colored with the kids (toddlers to 10-year-olds, 12 to 15 in number), painted faces, and played games with them. Each day, the number of children within the group increased. She was ecstatic in the evenings, describing each child as she held the pictures they had colored for her. We flew back on Saturday and returned to our home at 3 a.m. Sunday morning.

Both tired and unsettled from jet lag and travel, we slept ... but still not well. I had been battling an upper nasal infection since Wednesday, and by Monday morning I had a fever of 101. Brenda had nasal congestion, but no fever, and was nursemaid to me. We were both doing a nasal flush to clean out congestion. On Monday, I packed and did final prep for a pre-scheduled business trip to leave the next morning. By Monday night, my fever had broken. Brenda had the same congestion, but still no fever. While I plowed snow, she washed clothes and updated our sons and her family about the trip over the phone.

INTRODUCTION

On Tuesday morning, my alarm went off at 4:30 a.m., as I was leaving at 5 a.m. I gave Brenda a kiss on the forehead and said the usual, "Lovin' ya."

Brenda, still in bed, replied, "You too."

And I said, "I'll call you later." That afternoon, she texted me, said she was tired, was going to bed early, and I should not call that evening.

On Wednesday morning, I tried calling, but she didn't answer. I tried again at 10 Eastern Standard Time. No reply. At about 11 a.m., she sent me a text: Is it okay if I call an ambulance? I am very weak. I immediately called the ambulance service nearest to her and then I called her to tell her EMTs would be there within 20 minutes, and I asked if she was able to unlock the door. Her speech was almost indiscernible at that point. She thought she could, then said she tried calling friends, but could not read her phone anymore and told me when she breathes, she hears bubbles in her lungs. I said I would catch the next flight back and we hung up. I was on a flight in less than an hour. I sent a text to my sons and told them I had called an ambulance for Mom but did not explain anything other than that I was on my way back. While I was in flight, my sons were calling ambulance services to find out which one had picked her up and where she was headed. They called relatives and initiated group prayer.

This is where God's providence intersects with my life, Brenda's life, and the prayers of those lifting her up to God. During my flight, I prayed and was led to enter this event in my journal. As I prayed for her recovery, her comfort, and direction for the medical team, the dark thought of, "What if this is more serious? What if she does NOT make it?" ran *through my mind. I immediately dismissed that thought and prayed it away.*

The flight lasted about two hours, and as soon as I landed, I texted my son: How is Mom doing and what room is she in? (I visualized her in recovery with an IV, in bed and tired). As I walked through the airport, he called and said, "Dad ... I have bad news ... can you sit down?"

I kept walking, asking, "What ... What ... Tell me ..."

And then he said, "Dad, she did not make it." Time stopped.

At that point I did sit down—for how long, I do not know. My son called me back and said, "Dad, your brothers are at the airport, waiting at the baggage claim to meet you." I still sat, and he called again, to remind me. I told him, this wasn't registering, trying to understand.

I did eventually meet them, and we grieved. I was numb, in shock, and now led about by my family. I registered at the emergency entrance, then they allowed me to see Brenda. This was not the way I had imagined. I kissed the same forehead as when I last saw her and said, "Lovin' ya," only this time her body was hours cold. I picked up her hand and held it, apologizing for not being with her or recognizing she had been that sick. I am not sure how long I stayed in the room with her.

The coroner read the cause of death as septic shock. A lung infection had spread to her kidneys, then to her heart. The coroner went through a list of "what happens next" with me, and soon after a nurse in a plastic suit and face protection ushered me into a nearby room to look for a comparative virus (which I knew I likely had the previous week but had been able to heal). The nurse told me I was run down and low

INTRODUCTION

on sodium, but tests didn't detect anything serious. I asked questions trying to understand what happened, why, what if, and for anything that could explain why my wife had passed. I would later learn that she had septic shock, which is often undetected by the patient and the hospital before it spreads rapidly. Meanwhile, I may have been physically okay, but I was still in disbelief or shock. I had no emotions yet.

Brenda Warnke

Brenda was born February 6, 1958, in Glencoe, Minnesota. She died February 10, 2016. We married on October 7, 1977. In the early years of marriage, Brenda's heart was focused solely on motherhood, and she felt blessed to be a stay-at-home mom. She introduced our sons to the hobby farm life of raising sheep, chickens, cats, and dogs. Her life was made whole by serving and loving every creature and person. I have pictures of her cradling everything from lambs to children in her arms.

Brenda had such passion for extending God's love to others that she often overlooked herself. She volunteered at the food pantry, made meals for shut-ins, brought the handicapped to clinics, and always played games and shared in fellowship with them. She loved her boys, other children, and her grandchildren. She often said her purpose in life was to raise children, which she recognized reached far beyond her own.

She passionately enjoyed cooking. Many knew her as a food critic because of her discerning palate and ability to dissect and re-create any dish. She always looked for new tastes, recipes, and exotic ingredients that she would search and find throughout markets around the world. When it came to outdoor activities, she equally embraced adventure. Brenda cherished nature and loved to support the local wildlife, including bears, deer, and birds. She excelled as the best fisherperson in the boat and typically had the most success on our fishing trips. She enjoyed the outdoors in every way she could: walking, biking, snowshoeing, and camping. She loved kayaking and paddled 125 miles in 2015.

Professionally, Brenda possessed experience in travel, accounting, documentation, and seminar development. She played an instrumental role in the formation and cohesion of the company we worked for. She formed its personality during the initial years, and I recall her phone conversations with clients always extending to the caller's family or their personal uplifting. Within my industry, many around the world knew her well and sorrowfully mourned her absence. She stood out as the one everyone recognized and preferred to talk to, with her smiling, warm personality, always next to me.

Brenda and I totally enjoyed and appreciated each other and our life experiences. We continually reminded each other of our love, our appreciation of our life together, and recognition of each other as best friends. We could counsel each other and talk for hours about our interests and concerns.

I write this without regrets regarding our relationship and wish for each of you to develop and/or cherish a similar relationship. Savor it, remind each other … as you know not the day, nor the hour a life may be called from you.

INTRODUCTION

Maureen's Story

It was a Sunday night; we had just returned from the Twin Cities that morning, having celebrated Christmas with my family on Saturday night. Chuck had gotten up early on Sunday and did some last-minute Christmas shopping—trying to hide a kayak in the back of the truck before we got on the road and headed home to Spooner.

It was a quiet evening; I was trying to get our Christmas cards done. Annie (12) was reading while Tyler (10) and Chuck watched football and played pinochle. Chuck left to go play basketball at the elementary school with a men's pick-up league.

About an hour after he left, I received a call from one of the elementary school teachers. Chuck had collapsed during basketball and was at the hospital. I told the kids that dad had hurt his leg playing basketball, and I was going to meet him at the hospital.

While driving to the hospital, I was still unaware of what was to come and afraid to acknowledge my own fear, instead thinking about how devastated his mom would be if anything happened to him, her baby. I remember thinking over and over "Chuck, don't do this to your mom—don't do this to your mom."

The only person at the hospital was the teacher who had called me. I had never met him before—he had recently moved to the district. A doctor and nurse came out to see me in the ER waiting room. They told me Chuck had died and gave me some water. They watched me for signs of shock. The teacher asked if he should call someone, and I told him some friends to call. I called my brother in the Twin Cities. I remember sitting in a chair rubbing my hands down the top of my thighs down my shins to my ankles and back up again—over and over and over. Yes, I was in shock.

I had the hospital call a friend, but they mispronounced our last name and said Charles instead of Chuck. The friend said they didn't know anyone by that name, so I had to call the friend and choke out what just happened. The ER waiting room was filled with friends. I took one of my girlfriends in with me to say goodbye to Chuck one last time. He was laid out on a hospital bed, already a little cold. I stroked his forehead into his hair and just promised that I would do a good job raising Annie and Tyler—I would do him proud and I would take care of them. I can still remember how his hair felt as I stroked it.

Then the time came to make decisions and break the news to my kids. Which funeral home? I looked to the crowd to help me—no one wanted to answer. Finally, someone could tell I needed someone else to make a decision for me. "Go with Dahl's Funeral Home," they said. Okay—one thing down. How about organ donation? YES. They would need Chuck's health history ASAP and would call me so organs could be harvested.

Then my phone rang—it showed up as Chuck Revak, and freaked me out a little, but I realized it was my house where my kids were, without a clue as to what was going on. I asked the crowd, "It's Annie—what do I say?"

One wise person said, "Just don't lie." So, I answered the phone and choked out that I would be coming home and would fill her in when I got there, and I hung up. I didn't say everything was fine. It was time to go. The coroner would arrive soon for Chuck, and I couldn't do anything else at the hospital for

INTRODUCTION

him. Now what to do with all the people sitting there with me? I said I needed someone to come to the house with me and pointed out about 10 close friends. I decided who would drive my car and who else should ride with us in case I lost it with this poor guy I picked to drive me. I asked everyone to wait outside until I told the kids.

I walked into the house and asked the kids to come to the living room. Tyler was still watching football—I don't even think he knew I had left. I said I had some bad news—some really bad news. Their dad had a heart attack and died playing basketball and I was really sorry. Annie yelled at me. "I hate you; I hate Christmas!" She yanked the tree lights out. "It's not fair; he won't be here for my first date, my graduation, my wedding." Tyler gave a mournful, guttural groan and sank to the floor. Then he asked if he could pray.

Chuck Revak

Chuck was born on September 1, 1963, in Phillips, WI, where he grew up as the youngest of five children. His mother raised him to be a hard-working and caring man with a love for life, family, and the outdoors. Chuck and Maureen married in 1996, and they lived with their two children in Spooner, WI, where Chuck worked part-time for the DNR and was a stay-at-home dad.

Chuck's passions were the outdoors and his family, and he combined those whenever possible, including hunting at the cabin in Phillips, river camping with his kids, pulling skiers and tubers behind the boat for hours, fishing with his mom, and running Cousins' Camp for his nieces and nephews every summer.

Life was a great adventure, and he lived it fully with a heartfelt smile for all he encountered. Chuck died on December 20, 2009.

John's Story

I am John Kidder. I'm a farmer, a father to five sons, and a husband to my beautiful wife Diane.

In 2009, my wife Diane received a cancer diagnosis. That news came as a big shock to us. My first thought was this would be another prayer victory for our family—another opportunity for God to show up just as He had always done for us. There were times throughout the years of raising our boys that four of the five had life-threatening events. We did our part, we covered them in prayer, and God showed up and answered every one of those prayers. In my mind and in my heart, God was batting 1000. I truly believed that God would see us through this health situation with Diane. We had so many plans for when we retired. We had a lot of life left to live.

Our lives had taken us in many different directions since the time we first met, became friends, and then married on July 12, 1968. Our friendship always remained strong—our faith in God remained strong, and throughout our short, short time together we had a lasting bond that we both recognized as a gift from God.

Diane died of cancer on October 10, 2014.

INTRODUCTION

For now, we are apart in body, but one day I will join her.

I will never forget the night she said goodbye. I knew her journey in our world was almost over, but she did not leave, and it was as if she would not leave until she said goodbye to me. The room had been filled with the laughter of family and friends, and somehow (must have been through the Holy Spirit), Diane looked in the direction of my chair, her eyes wide open, and she smiled at me. I moved quickly to her bedside and wrapped my arms around her. She spoke softly, "see you ..." and I finished her sentence, "... on the other side." Such a peaceful look came over her face as I watched her leave our world behind.

I was numb and in shock. I felt God had let us down by not answering our prayers. I was alone while she was now with God. I talked to our pastor about our prayers not being answered; he replied that God did not answer Jesus' prayer when he implored, "Let this cup pass from me."

Over the first four months, I remained numb and in shock as I retreated into myself. I built walls around my heart, around my emotions. I kept myself busy to occupy my thoughts and time. But this only brought me temporary relief while trying to avoid the pain and loneliness. My emotions would eventually erupt; they would flow without warning, washing over me like waves tossing me back and forth. I attended a grief support group in another town with people I did not know. I listened to their stories of loss and shared mine while realizing how important it is to talk about our losses. One thing stood out to me, even though I still grieved so deeply: a sense of calm had come over me knowing that Diane had peace. Not everyone has that assurance of hope. I recognized their lack of peace, and I believe some recognized my abundance. I am thankful for this first group I attended, as I have found support to be necessary for healing, but I didn't feel it was the right group for me.

Eighteen months after Diane's death, my local church began a grief group. Grief is a journey that no one can do for you, but the understanding and friendship that others can offer when they have also experienced loss is tremendous. Sharing a common faith turned out to be more valuable to healing than I could have ever imagined. Support doesn't necessarily come from the people you would expect it to come from, but it does come from family, from friends, from new friends, and from the Holy Spirit. You just have to recognize it and be thankful.

Diane Estebo Kidder

Diane was born January 25, 1950, in Buffalo Center, Iowa. She was raised on a dairy farm and was the oldest of five kids. Diane had a very difficult childhood and suffered a lot of verbal and emotional abuse. The only way she survived during this time was by crying out to God through prayer. Through these times, Diane learned at a very young age how to lean on the loving arms of Christ, the beginning of her relationship with the Lord. Her freshman year of high school, Diane had a bad experience that left her not trusting anyone. She turned to the only source of comfort she knew: the loving, safe arms of her Heavenly Father.

INTRODUCTION

In the spring of Diane's sophomore year, her family moved to Belvidere, Illinois, hoping that by selling the farm, everything would change at home, and it did for a while. On a cold and windy day in late fall, while driving to school, I saw this girl carrying her saxophone and books. I asked her if she would like a ride. I introduced myself, but Diane already knew all about me and who I was. After that day, Diane became known as "Kidder's Gal." Needless to say, little did I know that marked the beginning of 47 years of a wonderful life with this woman.

Diane and I married on July 12, 1969. We moved to Shell Lake, Wisconsin, to raise our family on a dairy farm. We have 5 boys and 15 grandchildren. Farming was very hard but also very rewarding. We taught our boys the value of family and hard work. Diane taught at the Shell Lake Elementary school for 28 years. She dedicated herself to mentoring and loving those kids, and it didn't stop there. Along with raising our own boys, Diane and I became foster parents to more than 20 hurting and lost kids. Diane not only showed them what a mother's love looked like but also showed them God's love.

Diane's relationship with the Lord was one of complete love and trust. Her strength as a wife and mother came from Christ. Diane always supported her friends and family members who needed a listening ear, a hug, or a prayer. People knew they could call her, and she would always offer encouragement and godly counsel. She would end almost all her phone conversations with, "Can I pray with you?" or, "Let's pray." That is who Diane was. I have no doubt her relationship with Christ began and formed in her younger years as a hurting child crying out to her Heavenly Father.

It was no accident that I offered this girl a ride to school on that cold fall day. God had His hand in our meeting, in our relationship, and in our marriage that was built on trust and loving one another for 47 beautiful years. Diane was received into the loving arms of her Heavenly Father on October 10, 2014.

Harriet's Story

At 35, I had never been married and had been toying with the idea of starting an inter-denominational singles ministry. A few years before this, I had ordered a gift subscription to the magazine Good Old Days for my grandfather. I had seen an advertisement in the magazine saying that they were going to publish a new magazine called Singles Circle. So, I subscribed to that for myself. It was folksy, written for and by singles, and it included pen pal pages. I wrote to a few people and maybe heard back once or twice. Later, I found out that when you are published, you are overwhelmed with letters. I had always considered myself an outdoorsy person but not into winter sports of any kind, so I always thought of January through March as the boring months. In 1976, I decided I would put my name in the pen pal section to fill this time of year. Turns out my letter was not published until the Oct/Nov issue of '76! I had been on vacation in Michigan and on my way back I stopped at home, picked up my mail, and headed to the Twin Cities for one more week of vacation. I answered the letters from pen pals that I had received but found when I got home that one had fallen on the floor, so I answered it and received an answer back.

INTRODUCTION

I wrote to several people, both men and women, but one person stood out as being very intelligent and articulate—and just seemed good. His name was Bill, and yes, he was the one whose letter had gotten dropped on the floor! Around the end of January, he sent me a cassette player, and we taped messages back and forth for a couple of months. On March 3rd, he called me at work and asked if he could take me out to dinner because we had never met in person. I replied, "How can you take me out when we are a thousand miles apart?" He explained that he had some time off and would drive out for a weekend. So, I agreed, and we set it up for two weeks from then. He made a reservation for one weekend at the Inn Town Motel in Spooner. He would arrive on Friday and leave on Monday. He worked it out and arrived a day early, so we met on St. Patrick's Day, Thursday, March 17th. The weekend turned into nearly two weeks. By the time he left, we were engaged, and then we married on June 4, 1977.

As we looked back, we could see how the timing, how our circumstances, and how our whole lives were directed by God. He had brought us together. We were 100 percent exactly what the other one needed in a life partner. We would often refer to Psalm 37:4 which says, "Take delight in the Lord, and he will give you the desires of your heart." Bill told me many times I embodied the fulfillment of his dreams even as a young man, and vice versa, this rang true for me also. God knew and orchestrated our lives to bring us together.

For about half of our married life, he battled heart problems. In 2007, Bill had triple bypass surgery and was sent to Hayward hospital for swing bed care. His lungs filled up, but by God's grace and miracles, he survived, and we were given eight more years. God gave us a new doctor that literally saved his life a couple of times. He remained in the hospital for six weeks between Duluth and Hayward. I traveled back and forth every day. It became one of the deepest spiritual experiences I ever had. I felt wrapped in a cocoon of God's presence. Though I had always had a strong Biblical faith, it solidified during this time, and I learned so much more of what God will do for us— presence, protection, provision. I had peace and rest and could get up and do it over and over, day after day.

At the end of 2011, doctors diagnosed Bill with prostate cancer that had spread to his kidneys and liver. He underwent chemo for seven months, and then treatment in pill form. In early 2015, the pill wasn't working, so they put him on a different one. During that spring, Bill and I were talking about Jesus, and he said to me, "Wait until you see Jesus, you won't believe Him—and I'll be there waiting for you too." (He could make this statement about Jesus due to a spiritual experience he had as a very young man enduring eight operations in one year.) The new pill they had put him on made him very sick. He had the option to go back to chemo, and he did the Friday before Memorial Day.

Unknown to us, he had a urinary tract infection, and the chemo made it impossible to fight it off. His last Saturday and Sunday, he would burst out into the most powerful praise to God I have ever heard. By Monday, he was heavily medicated and unresponsive. I had prayed for a long time that I would be with him when the end came. God woke me up at about midnight, and between 12:10 and 12:20 a.m., I watched as Bill slipped into eternity with God.

INTRODUCTION

I buried him on our 38th wedding anniversary. At first, I questioned the timing of this. Then I thought back to our wedding ceremony and the words we had chosen for that day:

> *Marriage Prayer for Bride and Groom*
> *By Dr. Louis H. Evans*
>
> *May they never take each other's love for granted, but always experience that breathless wonder that exclaims,*
>
> *"Out of all this world, you have chosen me." When life is done and the sun is setting, may they be found then as now, hand in hand, still thanking God for each other.*
>
> *May they serve You happily, faithfully, together, until at last one shall lay the other into the arms of God.*
>
> *Wedding Prayer*
> *By Fern Glasgow Dunlap*
>
> *Oh, God until we reach life's ebbing tide, may we in perfect Love and Peace abide, and when life's sun shall set beyond the hill, may we go hand in hand, together still.*

And the prayers were answered.

Grief is a journey, and some days the road is rougher than others. But God walks it with us. The first weeks and months, the song "Because He Lives" by Bill and Gloria Gaither became my encouragement.

Bill's favorite verse while in the hospital that last time, which we often quoted to each other was John 11:26, "And whoever lives by believing in me will never die. Do you believe this?" The cassettes from our pen pal days became "God's gift" to me in the early weeks after Bill's passing. Thirty-eight years later they still played, and I told my brother, "I felt like I was being courted again."

I know my grief journey would have been even rougher if I didn't know Jesus as my personal Savior. Knowing that Bill also knew Him brought me comfort and peace. My faith is strong and has been the greatest comfort and strength I could have ever had. I have even learned that the praise and thanksgiving to God for the wonderful man and marriage He gave to me is another source of comfort. The Grief Support Group has been a wonderful source of help, encouragement, and healing. I would recommend it to anyone who is faced with this journey.

William Carl Perry

William "Bill" Perry was born February 9, 1934, in the small coal mining town of Nanticoke, Pennsylvania, in the Allegheny mountains to Carl and Irmal Perry. He was the oldest of three, having a younger brother and sister. His father and several uncles were coal miners. As

INTRODUCTION

the coal mines began to empty out, his family, along with his uncles and their families, moved to Jamestown, New York.

This was an industrial city with lots of factories and work opportunities, but as an early teen, it was not a happy move for him. It had a different lake effect climate, and he missed the mountains. He never really liked New York, but settled there, raised two boys, and found himself single again.

As a boy, he had gone to Sunday school at a small Primitive Methodist Church in Nanticoke. He didn't learn what it meant to be "born again" as a child even though he "had somewhat of a relationship with God." However, at age 32, during a tent revival event in Jamestown, he was born again, and from then on, he had a growing relationship with the Lord.

Bill had many interests—gardening, reading, painting with oils and acrylics, making clocks, building his own home, and enjoying the outdoors. He went to be with his Lord and Savior on June 2, 2015.

Burt and Jill's Story

I am here to tell you about our oldest son Tyler. Tyler was born on September 27, 1996, in Fridley, Minnesota. His brother Adam was born April 14, 1999, in Saint Paul, Minnesota. They both enjoyed their bond, and how much they cared for each other really showed. Tyler was very protective of his younger brother and always watched his back, and Adam always looked up to Tyler. In their teen years, they enjoyed playing Xbox all the time.

During his senior year of high school, Tyler attended prom. He had a great time and wanted to stay for the afterparty and lock-in. He was so excited about this and so we agreed to allow him to stay. The following morning, we found much more than we bargained for about what went on at this "lock-in." The things he told me were incredible. Tyler told me there was beer, liquor, pot; anything you wanted was there and available that night. I felt shock and disgust that all this took place under adult supervision at a venue intended to be a safe place for students after prom.

The next day, nothing appeared to be out of the ordinary. Tyler seemed normal and wanted to go to a party with some of his friends. I said, "Play it safe and legal, but if you do need a ride home, call me." Tyler was a good kid, and we had good communication, so he openly told me the next day what took place at that party. I remember he told me that they had just about anything you wanted there, and a student's father, a respected member of the community, provided the alcohol. I could not believe the things I heard.

I didn't recognize it at the time, but this marked the beginning of change, perhaps the beginning of the end. It seemed Tyler was making new friends, friends that liked the "new" Tyler, and I imagine he liked this new part of his life, this new popularity.

We had a busy summer planned. After graduation, Tyler and his younger brother Adam went to see family near Los Angeles for a couple of weeks. They were home for only one week when Adam left for a week of church camp. Two days after Adam returned, we took a family trip out to Colorado to see our extended family. We returned to our small town 10 days later. Over the next five days, Tyler did the usual things: saw friends, played Xbox, and prepared for college.

INTRODUCTION

Friday morning Tyler woke up and was not feeling well; he had a stomachache and was looking pale. We mentioned to him about going into urgent care, but he said he was feeling a little better. He wanted to run errands with us, then his appetite came back, and he took a nap that afternoon. We thought it was a little bug in his system, and that it would pass. That evening, he really wanted to go to his friend's house to play Xbox all night.

On Saturday July 11, 2015, everything changed, everything stopped. I mean everything. Time stood still. People were motionless, objects didn't move. At about 10:30 a.m., the doorbell rang. I thought it was Tyler coming home from the Xbox party at his friend's house. This was far from reality as I grasped the door handle and gave it a fast twist. Opening the door, I could see a policeman standing in front of me. He asked my name and if Tyler was my son. Fear gripped me as I identified myself and said, "Yes, Tyler is my son." He asked me very quietly if I would like to sit down. Flashbacks flooded me from my military days; I knew what this meant. I had seen this scenario hundreds of times before. But the words the officer spoke next ... I couldn't hear, or maybe I refused to hear. I could only see him mouthing the words, "Your son is dead." I could not process what he said, but the words kept getting louder inside my head. "Your son is dead, YOUR SON IS DEAD, YOUR SON IS DEAD ... Your ... son ... is ... dead."

I stood motionless in the living room. The officer right next to me just stared at me, probably wondering if I would pass out or go into shock. My heart broke at the thought of telling my wife Jill. She had gone shopping at the local Shopko and would be home soon. I worried about telling her. When she returned and received the news, she cried and wept. I wanted to shield her from this pain, but I could not.

As this happened in our living room, our younger son Adam was preparing to march with the band in the local, annual rodeo parade. He knew what transpired that morning, yet somehow, he still managed to play the same bass drum in the band, the one that Tyler had played the previous year. Adam marched the entire route. He told only a few people the news he had just received about his brother's death. He told the band director, "I did this for my brother Tyler." We were so proud of Adam for the amazing amount of strength and courage that he showed in the face of his pain and loss.

It wasn't until months later, when the toxicology report came back, that we found out the shocking cause of his death. Tyler had died of an accidental overdose of two prescription medications. We give our kids life and raise them as best we can, but nothing can prepare us for this kind of news.

Tyler Groenheim

Tyler Michael Groenheim was born on September 27, 1996, to Burt and Jill Groenheim. Tyler was a shy and compassionate young man who was always kind to others. Computers fascinated him and he loved the challenge of the creativity involved in programming. He did volunteer work both his junior and senior year in the Tech Department. He earned the "Most Tech Savvy" award his senior year. He also

worked at the local art gallery to help them with their online presence. Tyler was looking forward to attending college for Graphic Design and computer repair. His hobbies included riding bicycles, traveling, staying fit, and hanging out with his friends and his younger brother Adam.

Tyler left us way too early at the age of 18. He had a passion for life, a giving spirit, enjoyed making others laugh, and wanted to help others.

Karen's Story

Thursday, July 9, 2015, started out as a beautiful day. Dutch had volunteered to be the shuttle service for me and my two friends to paddle the Namekagon River. He dropped us off and met us at the ending spot two hours later. We spent the rest of the day doing maintenance in the garden and raspberry patch. It was a very normal day of doing life together.

As we were preparing for bed that evening, Dutch started experiencing stroke symptoms: slurred speech, mouth drooping, and mobility issues on the left side. I called my neighbors to come and help me get him in the car. When the neighbors arrived, they urged me to call an ambulance. Dutch was unable to walk or help us get him in the car. He was a big guy so carrying him was not an option. Once the ambulance arrived, the EMTs loaded him, and we left for the local hospital. My neighbors, who I now introduce as my personal first responders, went with me to the hospital; one of them even lent me their jacket because the air conditioning was so cold. I wore that every day in the hospital.

Once in the ER, it was clear that Dutch needed to be airlifted to Duluth, Minnesota, to a much larger hospital. I was so clueless as to the severity of it because I never thought this might take him.

Three things happened that seemed as if the Lord was trying to prepare me for what was coming. First, a member of the ambulance crew came up to me after finishing their report and held my hand. He said, "I sure hope your husband makes it." Second, as I drove up to Duluth alone at midnight, I listened to a Christian radio station. The song "Even If" by Kutless came on. I had never heard it before, but the lyrics just hit me. They referenced life falling apart, unfulfilled dreams, and how God remains faithful even if healing doesn't occur.

All I could do was pray that this song was not meant for me. Little did I know that our granddaughter would sing this at his funeral. The third encounter that God arranged to get my attention was a nurse who handed me a binder that spelled out the different kinds of strokes and what to expect. The book clearly stated that Dutch's stroke was most often fatal.

About 12 hours after Dutch was admitted to the hospital, a doctor and a chaplain wanted to meet with me. Thankfully I wasn't alone. Three dear friends listened along with me as I received the news that there was no hope. I remember thinking, "I don't understand. He was perfectly fine just hours ago. He is at a highly regarded hospital. This should not be happening."

I made a bed for myself on a little cot beside his bed in ICU, staying with him as much as I could, not wanting to waste any minutes we had left together. Family and friends began gathering to say their goodbyes. His son and family made

INTRODUCTION

it in from Germany, where they lived. Dutch began with normal communication skills and over the next five days, we saw him gradually lose the ability to communicate. He never experienced pain or anxiety. When I look back on those days, one of the greatest blessings we experienced was our time together to say goodbye and I love you. That is a treasure I hold dear.

Dutch passed away very peacefully about 1:30 a.m. I walked down the hallway on my way out of the hospital, and the reality hit me that I am no longer the same person. It was as if I could feel my heart breaking. The pain and fear of it all felt unbearable. I wasn't sure who I was without Dutch, but I was very sure I didn't want to travel down this road alone. Somehow during all these overwhelming emotions, a peace came over me. I remembered the scripture of Deuteronomy 31:8, "He will never leave you nor forsake you." I had always leaned into that verse, and now more than ever needed to trust that my God would be with me even through this heart-wrenching season.

The funeral was kind of a blur, but I do remember the hundreds of people who came. The sanctuary of the church was filled with old friends, new friends, and family. I stood for hours greeting everyone. The presence of so many people from every season of Dutch's life encouraged me greatly... so much so that I often tell people that the gift of your presence at a memorial service is truly the best gift you can give a grieving family.

While Dutch was in the hospital a dear friend had called. She told me to watch for God's blessings to show up in surprising ways. Many things transpired over the next months and years where I could see God's hand at work, feel His nearness, experience peace in the devastation, and see relationships mend. Psalms 34:18 says, "The Lord is close to the brokenhearted and saves those who are crushed in spirit." Our God is faithful to walk with us through even the unimaginable pain. I have been blessed to see goodness grow even out of these ashes.

Dutch Huebschman

Merlin "Dutch" Huebschman was born on July 26, 1934, on a dairy farm in eastern Wisconsin. He was the youngest of three children. In high school he loved his woodworking classes. His plan was to become a tech ed teacher. Near the time of graduation, he felt called to ministry. His love for woodworking continued throughout his life. During his college years, he married his first wife, and they had four children. Tragically, three of his children preceded him in death.

After finishing college and seminary, Dutch pastored two churches in Cleveland, Wisconsin, for eight years. He joined the Navy as a chaplain in 1967. This meant a tour of duty in Vietnam, where he served with the Marines during the 1968 Tet Offensive. Dutch retired from the service after 21 years. Dutch then again pastored two churches in western Wisconsin.

Dutch and I met in Argentia, Newfoundland, on August 9, 1981. He had arrived at the US Navy base in July to serve as the Protestant chaplain. I arrived on August 9th to teach third and fourth grade children of the sailors stationed there. Dutch was very warm, friendly, and truly loved people. Hurting people gravitated toward him because he exuded compassion and kindness.

Our relationship began as a friendship in which we enjoyed shared activities like racquetball, tennis, ice skating, and hiking. There was a 20-year age difference between us. He was a truly kind friend. It wasn't long before any misgivings about age melted away. After a few months we were engaged and then married on July 10, 1982.

Dutch was a "prince of a fellow," as one friend described him. His kind heart and self-sacrificing nature drew people to him.

"People are most important," was a sentence I often heard from him. When prioritizing life, it was the needs of people that tipped the scale and moved him.

Our life together led to several places before bringing us to northwest Wisconsin. In June of 2000, we moved permanently to our lake home. We enjoyed biking, fishing, traveling, and swimming in the summer and snowshoeing and cross-country skiing in the winter. We enjoyed entertaining friends and hosting his children and grandchildren any time we were able to have them. On July 15, 2015, Dutch went peacefully from this world into the arms of his Lord.

Writing ... Your Story

We hope that by reading our stories you will be inspired to write your own. We have provided a place at the end of this book for you to start writing your story of loss. It is no small task. There are tears and pain in recounting the details. The emotions that accompany each detail are draining, and pouring them out on paper is exhausting.

The stories we have written may be difficult for our families to read. But we write our stories to release the pain, to untangle the unspoken emotional turmoil as we lived it and as we saw it. Everyone, even our families, has their own story to tell.

For our publication purposes, I asked my youngest daughter if she would give our individual stories an initial proofread. My daughter knew almost everyone in the group from the social gatherings in our home. She knew Burt and Jill's son from school, and she had also become good friends with Maureen's daughter while in high school. She agreed to read each of the stories. With each one she read she would text me and say something like, "I just read Maureen's story. I didn't know all the details. Mom, it was so sad."

To which I would quietly reply, "I know, honey." This went on all afternoon as she would read and then text me a similar message on the sadness of the story. I finally said to her, "Honey, this is a grief book; they are all going to be sad." She knew that, of course, but raw emotion cuts deep. She told me she had decided to save my story for last. When no phone call or text message came, I finally called her that evening and asked, "Well, what about my story?"

I understood when my daughter quietly replied, "I couldn't read it, Mom. I'm sorry, it's just too hard."

I wonder if the reason we hold onto the memories of the event—replaying them over and over and tormenting ourselves—is out of some sort of fear that we might forget. However, there is healing in the telling of our story, even if no one reads it. There is release from the torment as the memories we fear may eventually fade are safely penned to page.

~Jeannine

*"No one ever told me that grief
felt so much like fear ..."*

~ *C. S. Lewis*

Grief is the price you pay

for loving someone...

ONE

Experiencing Grief

"I am feeble and utterly crushed; I groan in anguish of heart. All my longings lie open before you, Lord; my sighing is not hidden from you."
Psalms 38:8-9

What is Grief?

Grief encompasses the emotional, mental, and physical suffering and distress over the loss of a loved one. Synonyms include sorrow, misery, sadness, pain, heartache, agony, torment, woe, desolation, or despair.

If you have lost a loved one, then you are familiar with each one of these synonyms as they ebb and flow in our lives during the first few months. We should also add disbelief, lack of focus, lack of concentration, as well as loss of sleep, loss of appetite, loss of weight, loneliness, and loss of relationships. Grief saddens the heart and heightens the memory. It seems everything you look at results in a recollection of an emotion or an event you shared with the deceased. Grief can be described as a roller-coaster ride—a slow climb to the crest; you are lightheaded and vulnerable, then the feeling of panic sets in as there is no turning back. Your heart and stomach are pushed up into your chest as you free fall, weightless and out of control. Such is grief. Each person handles the ride—and the pain—differently, depending on their relationship to the deceased and the events leading up to the death. Some will not acknowledge it, some will blame, some will disconnect. The hope is that we all come out on the other side stronger and more compassionate.

The Beginning

The first day, first weeks, first several months, or even longer after the death of a loved one are often spent in what can best be described as a "fog." We can still function—get out of bed, make meals, even go to work—but it's just the process of going through the motions. It can be difficult to complete even the simplest of tasks, as our brain can seem sluggish. We lose track of time; we forget names of acquaintances or where we just set something down. During the first few months we will experience feelings referred to as "restless angst": the inability to sleep, getting up and wandering into other rooms, being unable to concentrate to get things accomplished, or feeling unsettled, aimless, unfulfilled, and unsatisfied. We may find ourselves searching for the one we have lost. Understand that these reactions and responses to loss are normal ... or at least as normal as anything can be.

> *"In the first few months after I lost my husband, I found this 'search' took several forms. I looked through all our photo albums, read old letters, listened to old cassettes we had communicated on, and searched for more of the same items in other places. Eventually, it became less acute."* ~Harriet

Even as we walk through this fog, we know that others are continuing with their lives. Friends get up and go to work the next day while we sit in shock, unable to leave the house. It can be hard to not get angry with friends, relatives, and even strangers for going about their daily business.

> *"I have such a clear memory of leaving the house the first time after Chuck's death to go to the funeral home to make arrangements. I sat in the passenger seat of my brother's car, and I remember being dumbfounded that other people were out driving around—like nothing happened. They were pumping gas, grocery shopping, and shoveling sidewalks. Don't they realize the world has come crashing down? I felt betrayed, even by strangers."* ~Maureen

Allow yourself these emotions. It's okay to be dumbfounded and angry but try to work toward some measure of comfort so it doesn't begin to fester. That might mean taking comfort in knowing that God is walking with you through the fog, or it might mean finding a friend to just listen to your indignation that life gets to go on for others but has stopped for you.

Determining your "new normal" is a phrase we often hear after the death of a loved one. Everyone's old normal differs vastly, so expecting your new normal to look anything like another individual who is experiencing grief is unrealistic. However, it is important to acknowledge the fog and the changes—physically, mentally, and socially—after loss.

> *"It felt as though my heart had been ripped from my body, and I stood there beside him, my heart, spirit, and soul bleeding—in agony beyond description, unable to speak. A part of me died that very same moment my husband took his last breath. The life inside of me felt as though it had stopped, but my body betrayed me—I was still breathing. I felt so small and so alone. 'We' were no longer ... it was only 'me' and I didn't know how to be me without him. Then the fog drifted in and settled on me like a cold misty morning. It felt as though the fog would never lift." ~Jeannine*

Phases of Grief

The fog is just one of many phases you will experience following the loss of a loved one. We have chosen to portray these phases on a pendulum because the journey is anything but straight. The pendulum illustrates our movement back and forth. You may move from one phase to another only to find yourself returning to a previous phase. There also might be phases or emotions that you don't experience or barely experience at all. Just be aware that the journey through grief is uniquely individual. It is not linear; it simply shares a common thread with others who are experiencing grief.

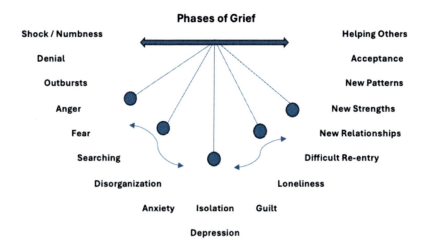

2025 Diagram by *Grace for the Grieving* regarding the phases of grief pendulum.

In 1969, Elisabeth Kübler-Ross, a Swiss psychiatrist, introduced her five-stage grief model in her book *On Death and Dying*. The stages include Denial, Anger, Bargaining, Depression, and Acceptance.[1]

She had based the model on her work with the terminally ill and it has been the subject of debate and criticism ever since. The model was mistakenly believed to be a specific order and that all people would go through every stage. It is now understood that these stages are only considered to be the most commonly observed among the grieving, but not in any specific order.

---

1 Elisabeth Kübler-Ross. *On Death and Dying*. (New York, NY:Scribner of Simon & Schuster, Inc., 1969).

Elisabeth Kübler-Ross has written numerous books on death. She and David Kessler co-authored the book *On Grief and Grieving: Finding the Meaning of Grief Through the Five Stages of Loss*. David Kessler has since written the book *Finding Meaning: The Sixth Stage of Grief*.

Defense Mechanisms

Losing a loved one is painful; many people try to avoid going through the grief process by applying some defense mechanisms. None of these are healthy. We are going to list some to see if you can identify with any of them.

Denial – People in denial often deny the loss entirely or minimize the severity of the loss. They refuse to talk about it or say, "Everything is fine," and quickly change the conversation. Denial can often delay healing.

Rationalizing – In rationalizing, we deny ourselves the right to hurt. We might tell ourselves that we shouldn't feel bad because our loved one is no longer suffering, and they are with God. While that may be true, we should not deny ourselves the right to feel sadness, because we do miss them.

Replacement – This can be anything that keeps us from facing our true feelings. Examples might be: pouring yourself into work, excessive purchases, numerous vacations, drinking, drugs, or an immediate relationship to replace the one we have lost. It is important to stress that replacements only delay healing, and unresolved grief will resurface sometime in the future. Unprocessed grief often emerges when we experience another loss which compounds the emotional effects.

Once we have processed our loss, a more positive approach is to reinvest ourselves in something new and positive. Examples might be completing an old dream or developing a new hobby. Many people who have experienced loss reach out to others to offer help and share what they have learned. Others volunteer for service projects in their community. Rather than thinking of replacing, it is healthier to consider reinvesting in something positive.

Some people get stuck and never seem to live meaningful lives after the loss of a loved one. It is normal to want to hang on to what we once had, but that can prevent us from embracing the future. Saying goodbye can be a healthy way to transition into the next phase of life. Some people write a letter or talk out loud to the one they lost. It's important to share what's on your heart. Share your feelings, regrets, lost dreams, appreciation, or whatever is important to you. This will often free you to move forward without them.

Recovery

Recovery does not mean a once-and-for-all conclusion to your loss and grief. It means regaining your ability to function as you once did, as you resolve to integrate your loss into your new life. Your loss will always be with you, but it doesn't need to incapacitate you. Recovery means you learn to live with your loss. It doesn't mean that your grief and mourning are over or that you are happy about your loss. Recovering means reinvesting in life, new relationships, new dreams and hopes, new sources of joy, and possibly new ways of serving and blessing others.

Obstacles

Some people struggle with the feeling of guilt for moving on after the loss of a loved one. They feel like they are betraying the one they lost. (Other people can make us feel that way too.) One way to address this is to switch roles. If you had died and your loved one had lived, would you want them to remain stuck or would you want them to move on to a meaningful life? Many people find this process freeing, allowing them permission to address the future with optimism.

The stages and phases of grief are a reference to help us understand what is "normal" in this season—what we might expect to experience as we navigate through these uncharted waters of our emotions. You might hit all the stages in the order depicted or skip around. You might move forward and then fall back. The hope is that, with help, we continue toward a place of peace. Drawing on God and His promises brings us to a light at the end of the tunnel—no matter how dim it may seem. However, do not expect your faith to allow you to skip through the hard parts of grief. God never promised we won't suffer, but He does promise He will be there with us when we do and give us strength if we ask for it. If we remain open, there are tender mercies that can only be learned during this raw season of pain.

> *"I refer to the early months as the Gethsemane Period when in Matthew 26:36–46 and Mark 14:32–42, Christ asked, 'Is there any way this cup (suffering/sacrifice) can pass from me?' I have now come to a deeper understanding of the Gethsemane story—the extreme agony and suffering of Christ, the disciples being oblivious to his condition, and the angels or Holy Spirit ministering to and strengthening him, while his followers slept. I have been angry. I would like to describe it as humbled anger or intense questioning toward God's intention and the suffering that affected me. I have questioned the need for this suffering."* ~Bob

Journaling

After recognizing triggers and dealing with grief in general, one exercise many have found helpful is journaling. This can take many forms. You can write letters to the loved one you lost, document what emotions you experienced that day, or describe your encounters with those around you. Journaling is a safe place to be real without anyone judging or feeling sorry for you. It's a place to be free about your feelings of fear, anger, denial, or despair. When we run into people after the loss of a loved one, people will ask us, "How are you doing?" We learn quickly that most people want to hear that we are fine, doing better, back to normal. However, what once was normal is no longer normal and that is something they cannot understand unless they have experienced loss in a similar way.

A journal can become your confidant, your release for the pain that others cannot understand. Even writing the words, "I miss you," is a release that leads to healing.

> *"On considering this topic, I went back and reviewed my digital (computer) journaling and discovered I had 23 pages of text before Brenda passed away. From that point until now (15 months after her passing) I have 43 additional pages. My inserts are short, with the longest being a quarter page. In my early journaling, I labeled each entry by a significant event happening in my life, but now I label by date. I see journaling as a way to question, to vent, to heal, to grow, and to praise God. I can read it, even when I don't feel up to writing or praising. I may read journal inserts to get through a difficult time, to uplift my spirit, or to get a progress check." ~Bob*

Discussion Questions:

1. Describe your feelings in those first moments and days after your loss.
2. How did you feel toward those around you?
3. What helped you get through the first three months? The first six months? The first year? Healing can be supported through memory and recollection of significant events.
4. How did you change physically and mentally in the beginning of your grief journey?
5. Review the stages of grief and identify the stages you have experienced.
6. Rather than deal with the pain of a loss, it is common for people to live in denial and act as if the loss never happened. Have you experienced denial as a way of coping with your pain? Is there evidence of denial in other family members?

Journaling Prompts:

1. Write your loved one a letter. Say all the things you feel you left unsaid. Tell your loved one how you feel now. Ask for forgiveness if required. Ask, "What could I have done for you?" Or apologize for not recognizing or acknowledging something.
2. If you could have one last conversation with your loved one, what would you say?
3. Be mindful to pray for others who may be struggling.

TWO

Extending Grace

"My tears have been my food day and night, while people say to me all day long, 'Where is your God?'"
Psalm 42:3

What is Grace?

Grace encompasses the receiving for ourselves and offering to others kindness, courtesy, and unmerited favor. Synonyms include mercy, charity, clemency, and leniency.

As we work through our own grief, it is important to recognize the feelings of those around us. We are not the only ones grieving. Others want to be helpful but often don't know how and many will make mistakes in their efforts to help. We will be put in situations that give us the opportunity to extend grace to others, even if their actions or words frustrate or hurt us. Extending grace can help turn bitterness to peacefulness and can go a long way in our own healing and grief process.

First Encounters

Eventually the fog will begin to lift, and you will start to interact again with family and friends. Your loss will still be foremost in your mind, and it will generally be foremost in the minds of those you meet. The first encounters with acquaintances can be awkward and stressful. Often, when you make eye contact with someone for the first time since your loved one's death, the tears just flow. You think you're getting your life and emotions under control, but those first initial encounters result in facing the shock of loss head-on. Acquaintances may or may not want to acknowledge your loss. It can be difficult for both parties. The loss story may need to be told again, and generally, retelling it comforts us. We are not ready to forget, and it can be healing to explain what happened. Each individual you meet will handle the sensitive issue differently. Some will be sympathetic, and some will tell you how they might feel if it happened to them. The latter may be difficult to listen to because it didn't happen to them, and you would appreciate that they listen rather than define it from their point of view. In some instances, relaying your story or answering their questions can be healing and in other instances it may be draining.

> *"I remember the hardest people to face were Londe's friends. I would see them mostly at our twins' sporting events and at first, I would come undone. I knew they experienced the awkwardness too. They would ask how I was doing, and I could see the pain in their eyes, as they would shrink back like they had just asked the wrong thing. It took a lot of self-control*

on my part not to cry until after I went home. I grew so afraid they would want to avoid me if they saw me cry and I needed them to be comfortable with me. They were like an extension of him, and I couldn't lose that too." ~Jeannine

A common reaction would be to separate and to distance yourself from social interactions. Another extension of grace is remaining approachable. Consider preparing yourself before you venture out to help make encounters restorative rather than exhausting. Before heading out to an event, think about who you might see for the first time since your loss. Imagine how you might react to seeing them and how they might react to seeing you for the first time. As overwhelming as the thought of this might be, it can be equally painful when your loss is not acknowledged.

Questions to ponder:

- *What are they likely to say and how can you best respond?*
- *Will they hug you?*
- *Are tears likely?*
- *What will you do if they do not acknowledge your loss?*
- *Should you assume they don't know and tell them about it?*

Responding with Grace

Figuring out how to respond is one of the things that can help us to become better rather than bitter. Friends, family, and acquaintances will struggle with what to say and many will get it wrong. Some will unknowingly say something hurtful (as you will see below in the examples of Gut vs. Grace); they too, are in uncharted waters. If something hurtful is said, it provides us with an opportunity to extend grace. This might be just by saying, "Thank you," and moving on. If you feel strong enough, reply in a manner that puts the individual at ease. Find a way to compliment them and even recognize their loss, if they were close to your loved one. Recount a positive comment the deceased made about the individual you are talking to. Kind words at this time can mean so much to others, and you will be amazed at how healing and restorative that can be for yourself.

> *"I had been grieving my son Tyler for 21 months and realized that there are certain moments that I may have a harder time hearing about death; I am thankful when I meet a person filled with kind words. This encourages me; it helps me to realize I need to aim to be the same kind of person—a person that lets the Lord's light shine in their life." ~Jill*

Not every encounter is going to go smoothly. In the early stages, you are extremely sensitive to others' comments, as you are truly vulnerable at this time of loss. People are going to say the wrong thing, and what might be the right sentiment for others may be the opposite for you. You feel that no one gets it—and you are probably right. It's not a situation many can put themselves in until they've actually been through it. Consider whether you really want them to understand. If they understood completely, it would mean they have gone through the same pain that you are enduring, and deep down, we really don't wish that for anyone.

Gut vs. Grace

What will people say to you, and how will you answer? Often you will want to just speak from your gut and say the first thing that comes to your mind. While this may be honest and truthful, it might not be gracious. The following questions and statements are some of the typical sentiments expressed to us by friends and acquaintances. We have listed examples of how we might want to answer from our gut, as well as alternative ways to answer which extend grace.

> *"How are you doing?"*

Gut: How do you think I'm doing? I just lost my husband/wife/child!
Grace: I'm taking it one day at a time. Thanks for asking.

They really want to hear that you are fine, but that may be the furthest thing from the truth. A better question would be, "How are you progressing?" but most people would not know to ask it that way. If you are not in the mood or it's not appropriate to go deep, then perhaps say, "I'm making progress." If it is the right person and time, don't be afraid to say you are lonely, sad, or just tired.

"They're in a better place."

Gut: What was so wrong with the place here on earth with me? I'm not a horrible person to live with.
Grace: Yes, I know they are.

Given time and a clear mind, we will probably realize the truth in this statement. Because of faith in Christ and eternal life, we can answer, "Yes." They are with Jesus … and nothing can be better than that.

"God doesn't give you more than you can handle."

Gut: God and I have a discrepancy on how much I can handle.
Grace: The prayers of friends like you are carrying me through.

Responding in this manner may be just the right reminder for them to continue praying for you.

"He is not in pain anymore."

Gut: He's not, but I am.
Grace: Yes, and it gives me peace that he is not in pain anymore.

This is true and comforting to know that they are no longer in physical pain or pain from the burdens of this world.

"You need to move past this. It's time to move on."

Gut: Ouch! The death of a loved one is not something you just get over.
Grace: I hope you never have to experience what I am going through.

No one can presume to know what is right for us. But try to recognize that because of their concern for us, they want us to get better.

"So, this is what you get for serving God. Why would He allow this?"

Gut: I can tell you don't know God.
Grace: Let me tell you about my relationship with God.

Not everyone shares the same faith that we have in God. Everyone's relationship with God is personal and unique. It is easy to have faith in a loving God when life is good, but it is in the difficult seasons that our faith is truly tested.

Avoidance

Even though some people might say awkward or hurtful things, at least they have the courage to interact. More often, people will avoid what is uncomfortable. They see us coming and look away or go out of their way to avoid talking to us. Avoidance can hurt, especially if they were close friends or involved with the events leading to the death. Sometimes we just have to let the relationships dissolve. A grace-filled option might be to reach out and put that person at ease. Most likely they just do not know what to say and are so afraid of saying the wrong thing that they believe saying nothing is the safer route. Try not to have too high expectations from your church. If they don't have an active grief ministry, they may not be equipped to offer anything more than a week or two of meals.

Helping Others with Their Grief

It can be hard to recognize the pain others are in due to the loss of your loved one. He or she was someone's best friend, parent, coworker, sister or brother, child, etc. As a spouse or parent, we may think we are the only ones hurting. Initially we are so broken that we can't see beyond our own pain and because of this, we may not recognize others' grief. Helping a friend or relative through the grief of your loved one can be a healing exercise once we have begun to recover. The last stage in the pendulum example is helping others—but try not to expect too much of yourself in the beginning.

> *"For my siblings, especially my sister Barb, I was a part of their healing. Barb seemed to need to be able to talk to me about Diane." ~John*

"The house was so empty every time I visited John. All I could feel was a huge void. I felt Diane's absence everywhere in every room. For a long time, I could hardly go there because I couldn't stand the void she left behind. Only by talking about Diane with John or our cousin did it start to bring some healing."
~Barb, John's sister

The Role of Tears

When we are grieving, we often avoid people and people often avoid us because we don't want to cry, and they don't want to make us cry. Consider this: Tears are the vehicles with which God has equipped us to express the deepest feelings words cannot express. Have you ever considered tears as a gift from God to express your emotions when you are unable to express yourself with words? Some people consider tears to be a sign of weakness, but most people recognize tears signify we have lost someone we cherish deeply. We never need to be ashamed of expressing, through tears, how much we miss the one we lost. Tears are the unspoken emotional connection between two hearts.

Many of us have learned that when our grief overwhelms us, crying is a release of the emotions that are pent up inside us. Many of us do this while talking with God. In Isaiah 53:3, Jesus is referred to as a "man of sorrows and acquainted with grief." There is something extremely comforting in telling God how much we hurt and letting the tears flow. Crying while we are alone with God is just another opportunity for Him to comfort us.

Sometimes after a major loss, the lack of sleep or excessive demands leave us physically and emotionally exhausted. During these times, we shouldn't be surprised if we are emotionally empty. "Dry times" like these are normal and seldom last very long.

Discussion Questions:

1. What are some insensitive comments people have made to you?
2. Can you give an example of how you wish you had handled a situation differently, with more grace?
3. How do we adjust as life moves on for the rest of the world?
4. Disruptive grace is an example of the conversation between Jesus and the woman at the well as told in John 4. That interaction changed the course of an entire town and the lives of many since. That which changes us causes us to refocus on people around us. How have you changed?
5. Do you think of tears as a gift from God to express your deepest feelings? Does crying before others make you uncomfortable?
6. How might you find ways to extend grace and be more supportive to others?

Journaling Prompts

1. Practice writing out how you would respond to awkward and insensitive questions.
2. Write a letter of apology to someone you reacted harshly to, even if you never mail it.
3. Consider sending a note to a family member that simply expresses "Thinking of you."

Hold on to faith; it's in the quietness that He speaks to the heart.

THREE

The Struggle with Faith

> *"You are my God; have mercy on me, Lord, for I call to you all day long. Bring joy to your servant, Lord, for I put my trust in you."*
> *Psalm 86:2-4*

What is Faith?

Faith encompasses loyalty and reliance on our belief in God despite our circumstances. Synonyms include confidence, conviction, belief, and trust. After the loss of a loved one, that trust and loyalty in God can be shaken. Many will struggle with their faith during this time and begin to question everything they once believed in. Even the deepest faith can be tested.

Looking for Answers

With the death of a loved one, we are often looking for answers and we want to know why. Why did this happen? Why did God let this happen? Why am I being punished? Why God, why? How often have we reflected and labored over the why?

> *"I questioned why. Would the world not be a better place with her in it and in our lives? Think of what she could have accomplished—the witness she could have been to others in the years ahead. She missed her first grandson's birth (six weeks later) and her eldest son's wedding (eight weeks later). Couldn't she have been here a few months longer? The circumstances in my humanistic view now appeared to be slanted against a loving God." ~Bob*

Unfortunately, there are no real answers to why and it's easy to believe that God let us down and abandoned us. A natural reaction when we feel someone has abandoned us is to abandon him or her. Many people struggle with their faith after the loss of a loved one. You may be one who has been faithful your entire life, you prayed diligently and attended church services, but then in your hour of need, you may feel like God wasn't there for you. Some quit going to church and quit praying. Some profess, "The prayers weren't answered before, so why bother anymore?"

It may help to understand that while God allowed this awful thing to happen in our lives, it wasn't His wish or His plan.

Many people will tell us that it is all part of God's plan, and we just need to have faith. God gave us free will and while He is an all-knowing God, He isn't an all-controlling God. He is not always going to reach down and stop bad things from happening to us.

> *"For the first six to eight weeks after our son's death, I felt very much alone. Oh, I had my friends, my church family, and others around me. But I felt so alone. Tyler died six weeks after graduating high school. How do you even comprehend that? My faith plummeted. How could my God allow this to happen? If He could raise Lazarus from the dead, then why not my Tyler? As prayers were felt and some even answered, I slowly began my journey back home to my Lord. It wasn't until I stopped looking for answers that my glorious return to faith came to be."* ~Burt

Prayer

Prayer is another area of our faith that we may struggle with after a loss. When our loved one was sick, we probably prayed like crazy for God to spare their life and make things better. Many make deals with God in these dire hours. And yet, the worst still happens. Then we listen to someone rejoice in how God answered their prayer. Their loved one was sick, and the prayer warriors took up the challenge and caused a miracle to happen. Why did they get their miracle, and we did not? How do we not make comparisons and feel like we got the short end of the stick from God?

> *"After Londe was given the prognosis that death was only a matter of time, a friend reached out with a set of faith CDs for us to listen to. I so desperately wanted to grab on to anything that could spare his life and buy him more time. I kept thinking, if we just have enough faith he will be healed. I felt this surge of panic as I prayed all night long for his healing. What if my faith isn't strong enough? It was in the early morning hours by the grace of God, that He spoke to me. If I continued in this vein believing that Londe's healing depended upon my faith, I would live the remainder of my life believing his death was my fault. God assured me that Londe would be healed, but it might not be on this side of Heaven. This revelation gave me the freedom to accept each day as it came and to recognize the privilege that comes from standing beside and serving the one you love to the very end."*
> ~Jeannine

We'll probably never understand why one prayer for healing was answered and another was not. Prayer is God communing with us, not just us petitioning Him. The act of prayer is engaging with God in loving fellowship. His effectiveness, as we refer to it, is not to be questioned, because we do not know the future or how it could be answered to serve God's purpose. If God chooses to heal some and not others, that is His choice. He created us in the first place.

We can be strengthened and uplifted in the knowledge that others are praying for us. It might help to focus our prayers not on asking God to make something happen, but instead to give us the strength to deal with whatever life may throw at us. Praying for strength puts us back in the driver's seat and can help propel us from victim to survivor.

When we can express emotions honestly to God, it invites Him to begin the healing process. He already knows how we feel, and when we verbalize it, He does His supernatural work in us. If we question or are angry—whatever we may feel—God is big enough to take it. His love and grace are there to bring us healing. This is His promise: "Come near to God and He will come near to you" (James 4:8).

When we question, "Why death and this grief?" we should consider the three aspects of our being: the body, soul, and spirit. The body is the way we relate to our environment, involving our five senses of smell, sight, taste, hearing, and touch. Our soul is the mind, our will, emotions, conscience, consciousness, and personality. At the soul level, we can laugh, love, and receive love from people in our lives, or we can be jealous, angry, and bitter toward others. The person's spirit is the inner person. Our spirit allows and leads us to communication and connection with the Holy Spirit of God. We are given sensitivity to God, an awareness of and relationship with Him. That relationship allows us to talk to Him and He communicates with us. We are open, in new ways, to understanding the Word of God and receiving guidance and direction from the Holy Spirit.

Returning to Church

Some may find it hard to go back to church. Walking back into the church where we recently held a funeral can be extremely difficult. The memories of the funeral come flooding back and bring us to tears. At service, we sing songs praising God, but we are not feeling very thankful. In addition, at church you are expected to be sociable and make small talk. Who really cares how much it rained yesterday when their life has been recently blown apart?

> *"I didn't find myself questioning God or asking, 'Why me?' I mean—why not me? But I did have trouble going back to church. I couldn't concentrate on the Mass, and sitting in the same place we held Chuck's funeral just led my mind back to the day we buried him—not one of my better days. Mass just seemed like too much time to let my mind wander. I had no choice but to sit and reflect and in those first few months, I just couldn't concentrate on the readings and the homily. I found myself with too much time alone with my thoughts, and I did everything I could not to cry. So, I quit going for a while until my mind cleared enough to focus on the service." ~Maureen*

Triggers

Triggers and flashbacks may also be referred to as "episodic memories" or in some instances, PTSD (post-traumatic stress disorder). Examples can be smell, taste, a view, a picture, an object, or an event that is similar to the past. Triggers can shake our faith because they bring us back to "Why?"

Church can be one of many triggers that we experience on this journey. Avoiding these triggers, although easier at the time, can delay the healing process. As you move through the different stages of grief and feel like you are making progress, there are times when you may fall backward. The key is to recognize what triggers a setback.

> *"Triggers are everywhere ... something people innocently say ... things we did together ... any reminder of the person we lost. Diane worked at the Shell Lake School for many years. As a memory to her, the school had a bench made in the school library. I had not seen the bench. But two years later I went to a girls' basketball game to watch my granddaughter play. At halftime, I visited the library just to kill some time, and I came across the bench. I became overcome with emotions. Things like this happen all throughout life; at first these brought me pain and a sense of loss all over again, and they would hit me hard. Eventually, the memories shared by others, the places Diane and I went together, and even the memory bench made in honor of her brought me the peace that the Bible speaks of—the peace that passes all understanding—along with joy and hope." ~John*

Some triggers are big events (i.e., weddings, graduations, important dates, and special places) and some are everyday occurrences. By identifying our triggers, we can be more prepared for the set back. Sharing those triggers with close family and friends can allow those close to you to be there when you might need them. Sometimes, sharing your grief eases it.

> *"One of my triggers, although I didn't recognize it at the time, was the produce department at the grocery store. Each time I tried shopping, I would get as far as the broccoli or the fresh green beans—and then I needed to leave the store quickly—before I had a meltdown. I eventually came to realize it was because Londe loved my cooking. He always appreciated my healthy, home-cooked meals upon his arrival home from work. So, I always cooked for him with great joy. That joy was now gone."* ~Jeannine

Rather than letting triggers crush us, we can try to turn those painful triggers into happy memories. If it is a date that is a trigger, try focusing on the joyful times of that date. It's easy to spiral down with regret that we no longer can celebrate with our loved one.

We question why and once again our faith may be rattled. Creating new traditions for these dates can ease the pain and foster a heart of gratefulness.

Some triggers can take us back to the death event—visiting a hospital, hearing a medical transport helicopter fly overhead, or reading a book or watching a movie where a similar scenario is playing out.

"One of the most traumatic triggers I have encountered was an inflight movie. The scene showed a father that looked into the face of his son, murdered, as the father watched, unable to alter the event. The scene and the face were an immediate flashback. It was as if I was looking at Brenda on the gurney in the hospital. Since the moment of seeing her, the expression of her lifeless face haunted me. I immediately hit the stop button on the screen in front of me. I almost became sick. My heart sank from 30,000 feet. I may have gasped out loud, because the person seated next to me looked over. I emotionally crashed. In this instance, I could only pray, 'Lord, help me, please ... please remove or decrease my hospital flashbacks.' I happened to be seated next to the window and looked out into the darkness and prayed into the heavens, for a long, long time, and then ... the pain lifted from me." ~Bob

This type of trigger can bring us to our knees. Turning to God and relying on our faith can carry us through these dark moments.

"That flashback tormented me for months. Then, while reading the book Jesus the King by Timothy Keller,[2] the Holy Spirit removed that painful vision and replaced it with a grace-filled one. In this book the author relates the story of Jairus's daughter in Mark 5:22–43, using the Greek translation of "my

---

[2] Timothy Keller. *Jesus the King*. (New York, NY: Penguin Books, 2011).

little daughter." It explains how the scene would have unfolded as Jesus took Jairus's daughter by the hand (she had been dead for some time). Jesus is basically saying, "Honey... it is time to wake up." This is spoken in the manner of a loving father who is softly, tenderly waking his sleeping daughter. From that point on, the expression on Brenda's face has been captured in my mind, as if her hand was held and God awakened her. That branded expression I have is now of her amazement. The hurt and pain have been replaced by praise. To me, there cannot be more evidence of the grace supplied to us, from a loving father, uplifting her ... uplifting me." ~Bob

Relying on Faith

This period of grief is probably the biggest test of our faith. It is hard to continue to put your faith in a God who has, in your eyes, let you down. The story of Job in the Old Testament gives us a great example of the difficulty of understanding why an all-powerful God would allow good people to suffer. God helped Job to understand that He is in control, and we need to trust Him even when we don't understand the situation.

It is important to note that not everyone will question God or struggle with their faith. Many rely on their faith to see them through their grief. Faith can be our best source of strength to help us deal with our grief.

> *"I had a strong faith before I lost my husband. It was the one thing that carried me through. Spending time in the scriptures, praying, and listening to the old hymns of faith were the strongest sources of comfort. Concentrating on the promises of the resurrection and eternal life was a source of comfort, hope, peace, and healing. Faith for me is and was a foundation."*
> ~Harriet

It is in the questions that we ask of God that He will answer us and strengthen us; we just need to quiet ourselves and listen.

> *"I continue to ask the Lord, 'Why?' But I realize I won't ever get an answer. Is it unfair? Yes, I absolutely feel it is. Yet, I have a choice: to let the Lord use my loss for good or become bitter and move away from the Lord. I choose to continue to forgive, which is a long process, and I thank the Lord that at least we had our son Tyler for 18 years."* ~Jill

Society uses the word "break" in the phrases "having a breakdown," "going broke," "broke up," etc. When we are broken, we often limit our perspective to the physical or emotional realm. There are more important questions that could be asked, such as, what is happening in the spiritual area of my life? What might God desire to do in my relationship with Him? How might He be using this brokenness to redeem, remold, and restore me to a greater wholeness in my relationship with Him?

Discussion Questions:

1. Are there any triggers that you have experienced that caused you to move backward in your grief journey?
2. Did you question why God put this suffering upon you?
3. How might God be using your suffering to strengthen your relationship with Him, or how can you use your suffering to strengthen your relationship with God?
4. How has your prayer life changed since you lost your loved one? Do you find it easier or more difficult to pray?
5. How has your faith helped you or hindered you in the healing process?
6. Review The Lord's Prayer. What is it saying to you about prayer and God's will?
7. Have you, or are you struggling with going back to church? Are there ways we can help you with this struggle?
8. Have you spoken openly to others regarding the difficult questions they may have?

Journaling Prompts:

1. If you are angry with God, remember He can take it. Write a letter to God and do not be afraid to vent any frustrations you feel with Him.
2. Describe your vision of someday being reunited with your loved one in Heaven.
3. Write down any triggers that have been especially difficult.
4. Pray for ways to uncover the questions that might be hindering the healing process of your family.

FOUR

Secondary Losses

"So do not fear, for I am with you; do not be dismayed, for I am your God. I will strengthen you and help you; I will uphold you with my righteous right hand."
Isaiah 41:10

What is a Secondary Loss?

Secondary losses encompass all the additional losses resulting from the death of a loved one. Synonyms include indirect results, consequential, and contingent. You would not be experiencing these additional losses had your loved one lived. Examples include the loss of friendships, income, your future as you viewed it, and even your own identity. This chapter will explore some common secondary losses and provide suggestions for dealing with them.

Loss of Friendships

Most people are not comfortable dealing with the pain and sadness of others. They do not know what to say or are afraid of saying the wrong thing. So they often take the easy route to just avoid the individual who is hurting. It is during these times of pain that we need our friends the most, and when they fail to show up, it is so hard not to become bitter. We see acquaintances go out of their way to avoid us and this can make us feel like lepers.

Another way to better understand avoidance is to recognize that people are at a loss as to how to approach us. It can be just as uncomfortable for them as it is for us. If we are able to extend grace, we can put them at ease and keep the conversation light. Often, extending grace is simply nodding and thanking them, when the reality is, what they just said or didn't say just plain hurts.

It is when true friends who avoid you that you experience the real secondary loss. If you've lost a spouse, some of the hardest friendships to maintain are the couple friendships. If you lost a child, the hardest friendships to maintain can be the ones with parents of your child's friends. The first time you get together with couples after your spouse dies can be awkward. It is so evident that something—someone—is missing and that the dynamics of the group have shifted. Some couple friends can get past this, but it takes some work and requires everyone to redefine their relationship a little. If you are interested in maintaining these friendships, you might try to help your friends understand that being with other couples, even though it may be difficult, is still important to you.

Even with all the best intentions on the part of your friends, over time you can find yourself being excluded from couple gatherings. You may suddenly feel like the fifth wheel, and this may amplify your loss. Or your friends may not want you to feel like a fifth wheel, so excluding you may feel like a kind option to them. This exclusion can be horribly painful and is another loss at a very vulnerable time in your life. It is important to recognize this loss and go through a mourning process. Review the grief pendulum in chapter one; you will need to work through the different phases regarding the loss of valued friendships. Hopefully the process will not take as long as your initial loss, but the loss of friendships is probably one of the most significant of the secondary losses.

Loss of Family

If your loss is a spouse, it can be hard to maintain the relationship with your in-laws. Family members are often not sure how to relate to you without the connection of their son/daughter or sibling.

> *"I not only lost my best friend, my wife, and my companion—I lost her entire family—the people who I thought were my family also. I have not heard from any of her siblings since her death."* ~John

If all communication had been handled by your spouse, it can be awkward to be reaching out directly to people you never had to reach out to in the past. Since the connection is now gone, communication can serve as a reminder of the loss and bring back all the pain associated with it. To avoid the pain, we will often avoid communication and just let the relationships fade.

> *"Brenda maintained the connection to all the relatives. She was the one who kept the birthday and special date calendar. Since her passing, I dropped the ball in reference to greeting cards and gatherings. She looked forward to having people over to the house and planning recreational events. I enjoyed planning these with her, as well as visiting family on their special dates. These ceased and I believe I recognized that loss about 12 to 16 months after her death. With nothing to look forward to, the house we remodeled to share with guests seemed void of conversation and filled with emptiness. In order to keep her legacy of hospitality alive, I started to invite church and youth groups over to share in our blessings and add voice to the structure and landscape. I still hold the title of the "tables-and-chairs guy" but now I'm no longer just behind the scenes—I'm the one who must initiate the gatherings. At least I still get to prepare for something." ~Bob*

Loss of Identity

Our identity is always tied to those we love: "Brenda's husband," "Dutch's wife," or "Tyler's mom and dad." When we lose a loved one, we lose part of our identity. We need to create a new identity or at least an altered one. This new identity will not happen overnight and is something we should always be working on. Those who were more independent before suffering a major loss may have an easier time with this particular secondary loss. For example, if we had a career separate from our loved one, we can often fall back on this identity to fill the gap while we redefine our couple identity. Or we may throw ourselves into our role as a parent, now that we have lost our role as a spouse. Or if we are retired, we may explore other avenues to fill our time, such as hobbies, social activities, or travel.

Loss of Future

We all think about, dream, and plan for our future—and our loved one has always been included in that future. When our loved one dies, the vision of our future also dies. Maybe you were saving up for a bigger house, or starting a business, or planning your retirement. While all your future plans do not necessarily need to die with your loved one, they will need to change. The future doesn't only include the big picture. Little plans will need to change too—the couples league you signed up for, the garden you were both going to plant, or the new furniture you were going to buy. Sometimes the little plans can hit us the hardest because we tend to overlook them for the big picture until suddenly confronted with one. For example, an email might come with the itinerary for the cruise you booked six months ago, and it throws your whole world off again, just when you thought you were getting a handle on the day-to-day stuff. We must rethink our future and develop a vision that no longer includes our loved one. It is probably the hardest step you'll need to take, but it is a critical one in working through the grieving process.

> *"Our 'bucket list' never got opened. Someday we would retire and do our bucket list. It is very hard for me to hear other couples talk about their trips or getaways, but I can't take away their joy in sharing their adventures because I am in pain. This is one thing I will need to work on and work through it ... I guess that is called growth." ~John*

Loss of Traditional Roles

While losing the person who cooked our meals can seem inconsequential compared to losing a spouse or child, it is just one more change we need to work through, and it can make life overwhelming. The different roles our loved one played are now unfilled. Who will change the oil in the car? Who will do the laundry? Who will help us make decisions—big and small? When confronted with one of these empty roles, we often just crumble under the cumulative weight of all that is now being asked of us. Sometimes we won't miss one of these roles until years after the loss of our loved one, and then it all comes crashing down again. This is where the pendulum of the grief process can swing backward.

"We had our defined roles, and it worked well for us; I never gave it much thought. But after Londe died, there were so many things I realized I had no clue how to do. Simple things like what kind of light bulbs did he use in each of the light fixtures? How do you turn off the outside water for winter and when? I didn't even know where to put the gas in the lawn mower or how to start it. Each of those realizations left me emotionally undone. I remember grabbing the shovel that first winter as I gave up on the snowblower that was too heavy for me to move. Wet tears were freezing on my face as I cried with each heavy shovelful of snow. I kept wondering where all his friends were who offered to help me if I needed something done around the house. 'I shouldn't have to call anyone to tell them it's snowing out, should I?' I thought of all the times he would go and shovel snow for the elderly lady down the street who lived alone. I had to remind myself that people were busy, and I needed to extend grace, not to expect anything from anyone and not to become bitter. How many opportunities to help others did I miss? I knew I, too, needed to be more mindful of others in need."
~Jeannine

Loss of an Income

Finances can take a drastic turn with the loss of a loved one. The first hit is the cost of the funeral and burial. Even the simplest of ceremonies can wipe out a savings account or cause the family to go into debt. The next hit is the loss of the income or pension our loved one contributed to the household. Not only do we need to figure out how to live without our loved one, but also how to do that with less money coming in. The financial burden can be crushing.

> *"Londe's five-year battle with leukemia took its toll on us financially. The hidden expenses of a major illness began to eat away at our savings. We went from two incomes to one. Then, unexpectedly, the month before he died, the company I worked for closed its doors. It seemed I had received a gift of time to spend with him, at the expense of having no income. After his death, grief left me paralyzed, unable to function in even the most familiar daily tasks. It was six months and an empty savings account before I could force myself to find a job. I needed to replace two incomes, and my new job didn't even come close. But it was a start, and I did it for the sake of my two kids who were still at home and still in high school. They had already lost their dad; I promised myself they wouldn't lose me, and they wouldn't lose their home. So, I forced myself to go to work every day even though I still couldn't sleep at night." ~Jeannine*

Loss of Concentration

As discussed in the first chapter, a sense of fog can descend on you after a loss. Eventually the fog will lift, but we may have a lingering loss of concentration or a change in priorities. What used to be important may not be any longer. This change can show up in productivity, maintenance of self or household, and in work ethic. This time may be obvious to colleagues; some may try to protect you or overlook it, and some may take advantage of it. If you recognize this secondary loss, we suggest you not try to hide it, but mention it to supportive people and your employer. It might be that your concentration is fine, but your priorities have changed. Before your loss you might have been a workaholic but after realizing how precious life is, you might not find work as fulfilling or important as it was before. Acknowledge any changes in concentration or priorities and share them with those who might be affected by the changes.

Discussion Questions:

1. Have you experienced the loss of any friendships or family relationships because of the death of your loved one? Would you like to share how you are feeling or dealing with these changes?
2. Changes in identity are inevitable. Sometimes these changes are positive and provide new opportunities, while others can be negative. Would you like to discuss any struggles or positive changes to your identity?
3. In every relationship, it is normal for each member to assume certain responsibilities. When we lose a partner, many of those roles automatically transfer to us. Would you be willing to share your experience in this area?
4. Are there ways we can help you if you are struggling or stressed with a secondary loss?

Journaling Prompts:

1. Make a list of all the secondary losses you have experienced.
2. If you have lost friends or family, you may want to write them a letter explaining your feelings about this secondary loss.
3. When you lose direction, find a way to redirect that loss. List some steps you can take to help you find hope again.

*Bear with each other
and forgive one another... ~Colossians 3:13*

*...as far as the east is from the west,
so far has He removed our transgressions
from us. ~Psalm 103:12*

FIVE

Forgiveness

"Be kind and compassionate to one another, forgiving each other, just as in Christ God forgave you."
Ephesians 4:32

What is Forgiveness?

Forgiveness encompasses releasing resentment, anger, or bitterness toward others or oneself. Synonyms include absolution, amnesty, pardon, and remission.

With the death of a loved one, we often feel wronged or cheated. In other circumstances, when someone cheated us, we forgave them in order to move forward. Determining whom to forgive after a death can be a little daunting. It might be something we don't even consciously realize we need to do, yet it might be holding us back. Think about whom you feel cheated by—it might be God, the doctors, the loved one you lost, family, friends, or maybe even yourself.

Forgiving God

Being angry with God is normal. We tend to blame God because He is in control of everything. He could have stopped this from happening. We might feel resentment because others have been healed but our loved one was not. Listening to someone state that God answered their prayers and the cancer went into remission can be hard to reconcile if your loved one's cancer did not go into remission, but you prayed just as hard. We need to come to terms with our anger toward God and realize He was not to blame and instead look to Him for strength and courage to keep moving.

> *"It took two years to totally forgive God. I felt a lot of guilt. So many times, I had to ask myself, 'Did I do all that I could for Diane?' The only thing I could do was pray, trust in the doctors, and trust in God. Through my prayers, I was learning to forgive God, which led to helping with my own guilt." ~John*

Forgiving the Deceased

We may feel anger toward the deceased. After all, we wouldn't be in this much emotional pain if they had just taken better care of themselves, made a doctor's appointment, not driven so fast, not been so reckless, or just stayed home. The list of "if only" and "what ifs" can go on and on. We can feel most cheated by our lost loved one because this was not how life was supposed to end up. In the case of parents losing a child, the parents were supposed to die first. We need to release the anger and bitterness we may be feeling toward a loved one. It is nearly impossible to move forward without working on these burdens of guilt. Total forgiveness doesn't have to happen all at once. It can be a lengthy process.

"When all was said and done—when I left his death at the feet of Jesus—I was able to really forgive Tyler. It took me several months and many attempts, but after I set it at Jesus's feet and didn't come to claim it back, forgiveness started to work. The new friends Tyler had made the summer of his death needed forgiveness too—so I did the same thing, leaving it at the feet of Jesus, and praying for God to release them from their bondage to drugs and alcohol, partying, and trying to fit in with their crowd." ~Burt

Forgiving Ourselves

We can have so many regrets after we lose someone close to us. Did we tell them we loved them often enough?

"During the weeks and months after Dutch's passing, I wrestled with guilt—the guilt that I didn't do enough, love well enough, forgive fast enough, or extend grace quickly enough to a man who loved me so extravagantly. At times, the guilt would be very heavy. I wondered, 'When I get to heaven, will

Dutch want anything to do with me? All things will be revealed, and he will know all the times my thoughts were less than loving.' One morning while praying and crying out to God a thought came into my mind. 'In Heaven, there is no room for unforgiveness, or holding grudges. That is all gone when you leave this life.' The time had come to forgive myself. I was not perfect but remembered neither was he. In heaven, all we have is love." ~Karen

We look for the signs and clues that contributed to our loved one's cause of death. Many of us become investigators trying to find out everything we can that led up to this tragic event. We talk to everyone involved, get second and third opinions, and re-enact the days and hours leading up to the death. We are looking for justification. If we can justify it, we might be able to accept it, and it might not be our fault. That can be a lot of guilt to carry around. Holding on to that guilt will not change anything. It will just hold us back and keep us miserable. Could we have done something to prevent it? We like to think we have control over our lives, and when something so tragic and painful happens, we believe we might have done something to cause it.

"I had a hard time getting past blaming myself. I took, held, and assumed the whole burden of robbing her life by not recognizing the severity of her illness. I felt I had robbed the world and God of her future capabilities. I searched and read verses on forgiveness and eventually understood that I needed to ask both

Brenda and God for their forgiveness. I asked (more than once) and eventually realized I was forgiven."
~Bob

Why didn't we make them go to the doctor earlier? Were we paying enough attention? Did we miss something we should have noticed? We were supposed to grow old together.

"Forgiving myself was the most difficult. I had an abundance of grace when it came to forgiving others. But when it came to me, I continued to beat myself up with the 'what ifs' and the 'if only.' I couldn't release that until I could admit that I did not control the leukemia that had overtaken his body ... I was powerless over death. ~Jeannine

There is no one harder to forgive than yourself. Recognize if your anger is aimed inward and work to let it go. Think hard about how your lost loved one would want you to be feeling. Sometimes it helps to switch roles. What if you had died? Would you want the ones left behind to be stuck in guilt and misery? What advice would you give your best friend if they were in your shoes? It's hard to have a conversation with yourself and this is a great example of how journaling can really be beneficial. Write yourself a letter from your loved one.

Forgiving the Doctors

If we feel the doctors could have or should have treated our loved one differently and we are fostering some resentment or blame, we may need to forgive them. Even if we know the outcome was inevitable, we might have some frustration or anger regarding the doctor's bedside manner or perhaps the lack of compassion provided during this difficult time.

Forgiving the Person Who Caused or Contributed to the Death

If the death was caused by others' actions, whether accidental or negligent, it might be helpful to find a way to come to terms with this injustice. Forgiveness is one option, but admittedly can be difficult to resolve, depending on the circumstances. If you cannot forgive, it can be helpful to just acknowledge that it will remain unresolved, and let it go for your own sake and peace of mind. Decide that you are no longer going to let the anger fester and continue to poison your life—instead, take your life back.

> *"It has taken many years, but I am able to forgive Tyler and his 'secondary' friends. Judgment and forgiveness are two totally separate thoughts that need actions separately. Judgment is what our God will do on the day we get to Heaven. Forgiveness is what we need to move ahead in life. Forgiving is when we allow God to intercede on our behalf in order to forgive."* ~Burt

Forgiving Friends and Family

Unfortunately, family and friends can abandon us when life gets messy. If we expect them to be there for us and they aren't, we can become bitter. Family and friends can include our church, our community, our coworkers, and anyone who let us down.

> *"I have a close group of high school friends who have kept in touch for 30 years. I host a girls' weekend for them at my home every summer. No one showed up to Chuck's funeral. With the exception of one woman reaching out to me through my brother, there were no emails or phone calls. There was a snowstorm the morning of the funeral, and they had a two-hour drive to my town. I waited for them to come up the aisle during communion and became worried that they might have been in an accident. I felt dumbfounded and abandoned—where were they when I needed them? In the days after the funeral, I became resentful and angry but then I started to get the whole picture. They were all up at dawn trying to figure out how to get to the funeral in the snowstorm and made the decision to stay home. It was the right decision. Many others made that same decision, but I harbored no resentment because they reached out and I knew why they were not there. I eventually talked to my high school friends one by one and came to understand what they went through that morning and all the calls they were making to each other trying to figure out how to get to me. That's all I needed to hear, and the*

sense of abandonment died—but we needed to talk it through with each other, as painful as that was, to get it right between us." ~Maureen

God has forgiven us of our sins at a huge price—the crucifixion of His own son. Jesus experienced a painful and horrific death because he loved us that much. While on the cross—he forgave the very people who were crucifying him. He said, "Father, forgive them, for they do not know what they are doing" (Luke 23:34). What a great example of forgiveness! We have been instructed to "Bear with each other and forgive one another if any of you has a grievance against someone. Forgive as the Lord forgave you" (Colossians 3:13). If you struggle with forgiveness, tell God. Ask God to help you and to heal you. We have been forgiven much, and because of that, we can forgive others.

One line of the Lord's Prayer reads, "And forgive us our debts, as we also have forgiven our debtors" (Matthew 6:12). We recognize that debt can be the burden or guilt we carry when not asking for forgiveness. Forgiveness can be asked of God and of the deceased for any guilt we might have.

No one is strong enough to carry a grudge. A grudge will always weigh us down until we finally break. Unforgiveness can destroy our health, joy, attitudes, and relationships. It is important to be honest with ourselves.

Discussion Questions:

1. Are there people you need to forgive? What is holding you back from forgiving them?
2. Do you need to forgive others face-to-face, or can you experience peace by forgiving them in your heart?
3. Are there any areas in which you need to forgive yourself?
4. Are there any ways in which you need to forgive the one you lost?
5. If you are sensing blame from anyone, what can you do to help them?
6. How has the loss changed your view of life?

Journaling Prompts:

1. If you are carrying resentment toward someone, write down all the reasons you are holding a grudge.
2. If you are carrying guilt related to your loved one, write down why.

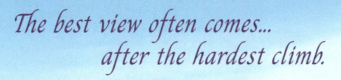

SIX

Finding Hope

"You will keep in perfect peace those whose minds are steadfast, because they trust in you. Trust in the Lord forever, for the LORD, the LORD Himself, is the Rock eternal."
Isaiah 26:3-4

What is Hope?

Hope encompasses the anticipation and belief for the fulfillment of things desired. Synonyms include trust, reliance, and expectation.

"Now faith is confidence in what we hope for and assurance about what we do not see." Hebrews 11:1

> *"Hope, to me, can be defined as being open to listening to the Holy Spirit and giving way from my plans to His purpose. One of my readings noted that we often pray from our will—our own predetermined outcome—when we should be praying from a neutral*

> *spirit ... as in "Thy will be done." Upon reading that, I resolved to carry on our love for serving and Brenda's heart for kids. Hope came to me because I could still hear God's voice. I found fulfillment by following through when prompted to work with a mentoring program for Washburn County and Timber Bay (a youth outreach organization in the upper Midwest)."*
> ~Bob

Eventually we all want to get to the point where we feel hopeful again. Death can crush our hopes and dreams, and with time, we want to be able to imagine new hopes and dreams. Hope is also defined as having good reason for believing that something good may happen. Where do we get the reason for that optimistic belief?

> *"One day, when I walked outside, something felt strangely different. I stood there for a moment looking around. Then I felt the warm breeze upon my skin ... I heard the rustle of the branches in the tree beside me ... I saw sunlight filtering through the leaves. I closed my eyes, feeling the sun's warmth upon my face. I breathed in deeply and the sweet, fragrant memory of springtime filled my senses. Hope stirred within me as I became keenly aware that I could feel ... even if only in that moment. I knew that one day I would feel again."* ~Jeannine

Everyone will find hope in different things and on different timelines. One of the best ways to start seeking hope is to look at those who have gone through similar experiences. How did they find hope?

> *"I guess you could say that I did not find hope, but rather that hope found me. I spent months trying to find hope in something, whether it was finding a solution as to why Tyler died ... wondering whether I did something to contribute to his death ... or reflecting on what role family had in his upbringing that made him do what he did. It wasn't until I became totally wiped out—physically and mentally drained—that hope knocked at my door. It was much like you may have seen in a picture of Jesus standing at a door, knocking ... and waiting for you to open it. That was me. I was on the other side waiting for Jesus to open the door and to let me fall into His arms. But Jesus wanted me to open the door, and He waited there, ready to catch me and carry me in His loving arms. God has put it in my heart to talk about Tyler's death and what it created in my life ... to share that with others. God wants us to share about His love and acceptance of us as we are. He also wants us to understand who we can become because of His love. We should not just keep this to ourselves but share it with the people in our lives and those we will meet someday."* ~Burt

Just witnessing someone who is walking through the grieving process and who still manages to feel hope can be enough to inspire us.

> *"While much time passed before I felt ready for new dreams, I did see a glimmer of hope in the days immediately after Chuck's death. I found we, as a family, could laugh through our tears. We could tell wonderful stories about him, continue to make a little fun of him, and comment on what might be making him laugh as he looked down on us." ~Maureen*

Faith and hope are interrelated, but not the same. Hope is active; it keeps us keeping on. It goes beyond optimism and wishful thinking. Hope enables us to persevere in the worst of situations. Faith is present tense, a foundation for hope.

> *"Hope, for me, is being able to see Tyler and be with him one day. It is also knowing that the Lord will continue to bring healing to me by His presence and that He will continue to change me. I am more open to helping others and sharing preventative material dealing with prescription drug addiction. I am continuing to ask the Lord for guidance." ~Jill*

"Hope deferred makes the heart sick, but a longing fulfilled is a tree of life." Proverbs 13:12

> *"It was Diane's birthday. I was very upset, and I could not settle down. I felt miserable. I went into the room where Diane died and while I sat in a*

chair, I could feel a very cool mist...a calming spirit. A gentleness passed through that room and my loneliness dissolved. God helped me through other lonely times as well." ~John

"A cheerful heart is good medicine, but a crushed spirit dries up the bones." Proverbs 17:22

"What does healing look like? Where do you start? Healing is a process, a journey, and it will look different for everyone. For me, it started with one simple birthday party I hosted for our Pastor Ron. Having a sheet cake decorated to look like a lake, I cut a hole out of the middle of the cake and placed fishing lines and poles in it, to make it look real. And real it was, because at the end of those fishing lines were live minnows. Boy, did the room explode with laughter when they pulled the fish out! I felt joy and laughter returning once again. From there I gradually started bringing more laughter into my life." ~John

Hope is an anticipation that things will get better. It helps to reduce anxiety, stress, and depression—allowing us to cope with grief. Hope contributes to our well-being, motivating us to make positive changes, driving us to carry on—in spite of what seems impossible.

"From the very beginning, I had a ray of hope ... a line from a Bill Gaither song, 'Because He (Jesus) Lives,' reminded me I could face my tomorrows. I

clung to that line from the first day on—through the shock, daze, forgetfulness, and 'foggy brain.' I even wrote it into some of the thank you cards I sent out. It became my lifeline ... my hope from moment to moment ... and day to day in those first three to four months. Gradually, I realized things were getting better. I began to enjoy some of my hobbies—especially gardening. Digging in the dirt, enjoying the sunshine, and being outdoors brought hope and healing to me. It unfolded as a day-to-day process ... the road to the new normal. Because He lives, I face each new morning, each new day, with hope and the knowledge that my life and my future are in God's hands." ~Harriet

Discussion Questions:

1. Can you think of some examples of how you are experiencing new hope in your life?
2. Did you identify with any stories shared in this chapter?
3. Can you think of other people who experienced the same kind of loss you are experiencing? How can you benefit from their healing?
4. After experiencing the pain from a major loss, some people are reluctant to dream again for fear of additional loss. Does allowing yourself to dream again minimize your loss?
5. Have you recognized any signs of unresolved grief in yourself or other family members?
6. One reason for a support group is so we can process our loss in a healthy way and develop a positive outlook for our future. How do you think you are doing thus far?

Journaling Prompts:

1. Write down examples of how you have experienced hope—even if it's just a glimmer—since the death of your loved one.
2. If the circumstances were reversed and your family was grieving your death, what would you tell them to do?

SEVEN

Identity after Loss

"Trust in the Lord with all your heart and lean not on your own understanding; in all your ways submit to him, and he will make your paths straight."
Proverbs 3:5-6

What is Identity?

Identity encompasses the distinguishing characteristics, personality, and spirit of an individual. Synonyms include individuality, uniqueness, personality, and character. Your identity is your sense of self, and without a strong sense of self we can become lost. Struggles with identity issues can lead to depression, anxiety, and other mental health issues.

Old Identity

One of the things that never goes away is that you were special/important to the one you lost: you were a wife or a husband, you were a parent, or you were a best friend, or sibling. The list can go on and on.

That identity has now changed.

If we cared for a sick loved one until their death, we could find ourselves without a purpose anymore. Our days were filled with doctor appointments, insurance headaches, and caregiving. Our identity is so closely tied to our roles in life and suddenly that changes. For us, the loss is immediate, irreversible, painful, and maybe even frightening. We are forced to think, "Who am I now and where do I go from here?" We become "the young widow" or "the parents of the teenager who died." This death identity is inevitable and while we may not be comfortable with it, acknowledgment of our loss is imperative to our healing.

Once the shock has worn off and we start to regain our footing, we may eventually find ourselves creating a new identity. This process can be positive for some people and very difficult for others.

Meeting New People

As time moves on, the death identity will fade and eventually you will meet someone—a new friend, colleague, or neighbor—who never met your deceased loved one. At first, this can be awkward. Do we tell them about our past? How much do we share? Is it necessary to share anything? If these new relationships develop, in time they may want to know, and you may find it healing to share.

The new person, on the other hand, may not find it awkward at all. They may be curious and want to know more about your loved one. They see you as yourself without having your identity tied to someone else. Making new friends and connections after your loved one's death can be a great first step toward finding your new identity.

> *"I was never one to suggest going out with new friends. I always leaned on Diane to do that. She excelled at it, and she was not afraid to reach out to people. Now I am more open to meeting new people. I now must step up to the plate and reach out, ask them their name, and not be afraid. Just like what my wife did. I am now learning from her. What a great teacher."* ~John

Finding the New Identity

One step to finding a new identity can be making decisions alone—especially if you were in a relationship where everything was shared and discussed. Start small; for example, rearrange the furniture. As you begin making small decisions about your life, you are slowly introducing yourself to the new you. A healthy part of grieving is to realize that you were not the one who died and that you honor the deceased by living.

You can't go through such a life-altering experience and remain the same person. Hopefully your new identity will be a positive change. Change is forced upon us. You might have to go back to work if your spouse was the main breadwinner. Other changes happen because your perspective has changed. You might become more empathetic toward others, or you might become more assertive. Many will realize that life is precious and may realign their priorities. Some create bucket lists or set new goals.

Working through the process of grief is exactly that; it's work, and it doesn't just happen. Time doesn't just heal on its own; we must be intentional to make our way through the dark night of the soul that we come to know as our season of grief.

When you suffer a significant loss, your heart breaks. The recovery for a broken heart is not like healing a broken bone or from surgery. It doesn't work like that. When you lose your life partner, you lose a part of yourself. You lose a part of your identity, and that can be frightening. The well-meaning intentions of friends and family who want you to improve, return to normal, and be happy again can often add undue pressure and hinder the process. They have their own idea of what your timeline for healing should look like. Others may come alongside you to help and be supportive, but it is you and you alone who walks this solo journey of the brokenhearted.

When we lose a person who is very close to us, we lose the interaction and validation we once received from them. Things that were supportive and comforting are no longer there. We find the hopes and dreams we once had will change. Over time, we learn how to live without the one we lost and eventually develop new goals and dreams. This is necessary for us to move forward in a healthy manner.

> "During my struggles with each facet of grief, sometimes—oftentimes—it led to a spiral of emotions that slid into despair, despondency, or depression. It reminded me of a line from the song 'The Sound of Silence' by Simon & Garfunkel. Darkness was my friend and I returned to talk with it again and again. I never understood the relevance of that line until I had to fight to keep my focus, to keep my thoughts on healing. I began to recognize that the darkness of depression began to feel as comfortable to me as slipping into a warm bath. The dark cloud that I once feared had oddly become a familiar friend, and even a welcome place. I had no control over my husband's death; I had no control over the domino effect of secondary losses that his death ushered in; I had no control over my emotions that could, without a moment's notice, throw me into an anxiety attack. But eventually I realized that I did have control over how long I remained under the dark cloud. Sometimes I was in and out quickly, and other times I lingered there. I think it's true in life that we can choose the comfort of the darkness and the familiarity of the sadness as a way of controlling something when everything else seems to be out of our control." ~Jeannine

In the early months of grief, you may not want to do anything or go anywhere. Family and friends will encourage you to get out and do things. They say it's not healthy to be alone. Some even dare to say that your life is not over and in time you may even find someone new to share your life with. You shut those thoughts down. You can't ever imagine that—you're not looking for that—you're not ready for that. And so, they worry about you.

At some point, you will get to the discovery phase of this journey, and you will start to desire new experiences. You might make a bucket list of new things to try or perhaps old hobbies to renew. Whatever it is you choose to do, you are beginning to take steps to find your identity or to create a new one, and you start to feel some excitement again. This can be liberating because you have something to look forward to. Be prepared that not everyone may be supportive. Others may seem to think they know what is best for you, even though they have not walked through the valley of the shadow of death. The length of that shadow is different for everyone depending on the circumstances.

In the book *Silent Presence* by Mary O'Shaughnessy, she made observations based on her twenty plus years as a bereavement counselor. Through the privilege of listening to the experiences of thousands of people who were mourning, she identified six patterns of grieving that occur throughout the process.[3]

- Absence of feeling (1–2 months after the death)
- Awakening (2–6 months after the death)
- Participatory Grief (6–11 months after the death)
- Hypervigilance (11–13 months after the death)
- Reorganization (1–3 years after the death)
- Adjustment (3–5 years after the death)

---

[3] Mary O'Shaughnessy. *Silent Presence*. (Deer Park, NY: Linus Publications, Inc., 2007).

It's all about processing and being intentional, not just to survive the experience, but also to come through it healthy and whole, joyful and grateful, with the ability to celebrate the life that your loved one lived and the life you shared with them. Once you decide to discover who you are and who you want to be as a result of this loss, it becomes a season of new beginnings and new possibilities.

One day you may meet someone who causes your heart to skip a beat, and the thought of dating becomes a real consideration. There are so many emotions to process. There may be feelings of guilt or betrayal of your deceased spouse. You weigh the possibility that others may question your loyalty or the depth of love that you had for your spouse. One thing that may help you during this process is to turn things around. What would you want your spouse to do if they were here and you were gone?

Your heart is only just beginning to mend and the fear of being hurt or hurting someone else is far more daunting than you would have ever imagined. So, you may ponder these thoughts about dating. You may tread lightly ... softly ... and slowly ... long before anyone ever knows you are considering this possibility and before you are ready to act upon it.

But what if not everyone is on board with you? This is a real possibility. You may have children still living at home or even adult children who are living their own life away from home. They may fear that they will lose their only surviving parent to someone else. They may feel that you are betraying the other parent. And so they may resist, through anger or indifference. Perhaps unresolved grief plays a part in all of this.

Once you allow yourself to be vulnerable and love again, you move into it with a different perspective. You have a previous marriage experience to draw from—both the good and the bad, as none love perfectly. You find yourself given a second chance at love and have the chance to show your love better, to redeem some of the regrets you may have, and to improve on some of the complacency that may have slipped in through the years. Not everyone desires a companion, but if you do and you are fortunate enough to find someone to share your life with, you are not replacing—you are embracing a gift to love and to be loved again.

"A new relationship could include cultivating old friendships, reaching out to others in their loss, or attending social events to learn about people. Some have looked for a new identity through education or by cultivating a new interest within their career. I realize now that I did all of those things. Some were intentional and some were to keep myself busy without expecting a specific outcome. Opening myself up led me to mentoring and supporting youth programs. Attending this grief group also surprised me because I found a new companion of faith and experience. She, too, had lost her beloved—five years prior to our first meeting within this support group."
~Bob

Discussion Questions:

1. What are some ways your identity was related to your loved one?
2. Share some ways you are creating a new identity. In what ways do you find this process positive and encouraging? What are some areas where you are struggling and finding the process difficult?
3. Has your loss changed your priorities in any way? Do you value things differently now?
4. Research shows that the broader the list of things that we use to identify ourselves, the healthier we are. What are some possible ways you can expand your identity?
5. Do you notice anyone resisting the changes you are making in your life? How does that make you feel?
6. Are there ways you could see becoming involved in community or mission work? This could bring joy and fulfillment to you and others.

Journaling Prompts:

1. Describe how you saw yourself prior to the death of your loved one. What was your identity?
2. Describe how you think others may currently perceive you now.
3. Write down something you could say to reassure someone if they are concerned about the changes you are making in your life.

Memories live within the window of the soul...

EIGHT

Keeping the Memory Alive

"There is a time for everything, and a season for every activity under the heavens ... a time to weep and a time to laugh, a time to mourn and a time to dance."
Ecclesiastes 3:1, 4

What is a Memory?

Memories encompass the ability of remembering or recalling images and impressions of our loved ones when they were with us. Synonyms include recollection, remembrance, and reminiscence. Memories are wonderful things that we can always keep with us, and they become so very important when we lose someone. This chapter explores ways of honoring those memories.

Experiencing the Memories

Working through your grief and moving on doesn't mean forgetting. You had the joy of loving someone wonderful and special in your life—why would you want to forget that? In the first chapter, we talked about things that can trigger waves of grief, and often those triggers are memories ... even good memories. You can suppress all memories of your loved one in the hope that if you don't remember, you won't feel any pain. Unfortunately, this rarely works—and isn't a little pain worth the joy of good memories?

Family and friends can be afraid to talk about our loved one after he or she has passed. They are worried they will remind us of our loss and make us sad. It's important to let people know that we enjoy talking about our loved one and hearing stories and other people's memories. If you bring up a memory first, it might make others more comfortable to do the same.

Another good way to keep a memory alive is to contribute to or even establish a charity in honor of your loved one. If their death sparks a passion or desire to make sure others learn from your experience, go with that. It could mean establishing a fundraiser to cure cancer, telling your story to others in the hopes that you can prevent another tragedy, or writing a grief manual so others can benefit from your experience. This type of action allows you to move forward while paying homage to your loved one and it can provide you with healing and contentment.

> *"One way we are keeping Tyler's memory alive is by giving a $250 scholarship every year at Spooner High School to a graduating senior who is interested in computer science or graphic design. Tyler was really passionate about computers. We named the scholarship "In Memory of Tyler Groenheim." ~Jill*

Physical Reminders

Many people find a way to repurpose the clothes of a deceased family member by fashioning them into pillows or quilts. Sharing your loved one's possessions with family and close friends can really mean so much to both you and the one receiving the item. It is something that can be cherished, which helps to keep the memory alive. Sharing and repurposing possessions can help make the process of cleaning out a closet or office or bedroom much easier to deal with. Instead of just getting rid of what you believe to be your last ties to your loved one, you are spreading his or her memory to others.

> *"I had a desire to make quilts or pillows from Londe's clothing for each of our six children, and I still hope to do this one day. This task honestly is quite overwhelming. So, as a start, I had a close friend help me to make an apron from one of his dress shirts and a pair of his jeans. Inside the pocket of the apron, I placed favorite recipes along with two that were handwritten by grandmothers who had passed*

years earlier. This is a sentimental keepsake that our daughter will always treasure—something from her dad and pieces of generations past." ~Jeannine

Goodwill or other thrift stores are one option, but may we suggest donating your loved one's things to a local church that has a mission outreach? A deceased person's car can be an especially hard item to make a decision about. It is probably the most valuable single item attached to one person. From a financial standpoint there may be no other choice than to sell it. If financial circumstances do not require you to sell, it becomes a harder decision.

The decision of what to keep and what to give away can be emotionally overwhelming and it needs to be done on your own timeline—not someone else's. Don't be pressured into dealing with possessions before you are ready. You also do not need to do it all at once. Take your time and do as much as you are able and then put the rest away for another time.

Significant Dates

We dread the anniversaries of the death, the birth, the marriage, and any other significant dates in your loved one's life. Rather than dreading the day and hoping you just get through it, try remembering the joyful times you had on that date. Often the anniversaries make us regret the fact that we won't have any more of the celebrations with them. To help ease the regret of missing future dates, remember the times you really honored your loved one on past dates—the time your birthday gift really hit the mark, or the extra-special anniversary dinner you had together. Use these times to remind yourself that you didn't always take your loved one for granted and that you were a big source of joy for them while on this earth.

> *"Chuck's first birthday after his death hit me harder than I ever would have imagined. Had he not died, we would have been doing something special that day—even if it was as simple as dinner and a cake. On that first birthday in his absence, one of his nephews said he put on a new pair of socks in honor of Chuck. (My husband thought there could be no better feeling than putting on a new pair of socks, and he always gave socks as gifts.) Then a niece said she had put on a new pair of socks that day too. So, a new tradition emerged. Every year on September 1st, we all wear a new pair of socks to celebrate Chuck's birthday." ~Maureen*

Creating new traditions for these dates/events can ease the pain and might even allow you to look forward to them.

> *"Anniversaries of any special date or location can be difficult for me. Early on, I was counseled to take those difficult times and look for the happiness within them. I attempt to apply that wise counsel (Thank you, Ruth). On the first anniversary of Brenda's death, I had to apply that counsel in rapid succession. First, I revisited the people and location in Nicaragua with*

Pastor Mike. This proved very difficult as I now walked alone, whereas a year before, I had held her hand. I listened as Myra told the story of Brenda visiting her family and the love transferred through her. After my return, Linn, my niece, prompted and organized a family gathering at our house. She suggested inviting local friends as well, which increased the number to 45 people. In order to complete this as an honorarium or memorial, I developed a slideshow for my talking points. These events were difficult for me, but I recognize them now as healing, a release, and recovery points. I am thankful to Mike and Linn, for prompting and supporting me through these challenges." ~Bob

Retaining Memories with a New Family

Not all people who have lost a spouse will be looking for companionship or a new relationship. Some people are comfortable with their life the way it is, while others may be hopeful to find new love. Keeping the memory of your first love alive will always be important. Entering a new relationship doesn't mean you have to suppress all memories and talk of your deceased loved one. However, having an open and honest discussion about what is comfortable for all parties is crucial in the blending of your futures together and the honoring of your previous relationship.

Honest Memories

All of us have both positive and negative qualities, and we all have the ability to bring out the best or worst in others. Some people put their loved one or their relationship on an unrealistic pedestal. Recreating that relationship into something grand and majestic and forgetting the difficult parts can make it very hard to have another relationship—anyone else may fall short by comparison. While you don't need to dwell on the bad times, just make sure you don't manufacture unrealistic memories. Healthy grieving involves an honest assessment of the one we lost and the life we lived so that we can move into a new relationship, healthy and whole.

Eventually our memories will fade, and this can cause us to panic. We can no longer easily picture their face, their smile, or their voice. Unfortunately, we can't stop this from happening, but we can be ready for it and know that it doesn't mean we loved them any less. If you have concerns of memories being lost, it can be helpful to pull out photo albums or digital files. This may not be comfortable in the early stages, but eventually you may find this comforting to review alone or with family or friends.

"I set up storage on Google Photos, which categorizes photos and videos by date and location. I found that finding and saving videos was the best way to remember how Brenda looked and the sound of her voice. These special moments in time bring joy and comfort to me." ~Bob

It is true that we shall never hear their voice, touch them, or feel their physical presence again. For this loss, our hearts are ever aching. But we will heal in the warmth of their memory, their soulful presence, and their spirit. In the beginning of grief, we are terrified that our memories will fade. Memories are indestructible; they are the bond that we have with our loved ones, and this is what colors our living now as we move to the other side of grief.

Discussion Questions:

1. Have you or others created a skewed memory of your lost loved one?
2. What have you done to keep the memory of your loved one alive?
3. Are you struggling with what to do with your loved one's possessions?
4. Is there someone who would treasure a specific item that belonged to your loved one?
5. What item is or was the hardest one to make a decision about (keeping or giving away)?

Journaling Prompts:

1. Write about your favorite memories with your loved one.
2. In addition to big memories, write down what a typical day with your loved one was like.
3. As others share stories with you, try to write them down so you can go back to them and remember the impact your loved one had on others.

Additional Stories of Loss

Loss Through Suicide

Suicide is defined in the dictionary as the act of intentionally taking one's own life. We all agree this is true—but it is so much more than that. It takes a piece of those left behind too. Some of my hardest grief experiences have been a result of death by suicide—my high school boyfriend, my mom, and several other acquaintances and students. Experiences like this are some of the catalysts that led me to my calling as a high school counselor.

My mom's boyfriend died by suicide on April 7, 1984. His death left my mom devastated and pregnant with their son Adam. As a nine-year-old girl, it left me confused and afraid as I waited outside the house on the steps, listening to her screams when she found him. I am sure she never recovered from that. Looking back, the day's events are blurry leading up to the police officer talking to me. I often wonder what the officer thought, having to explain suicide to a little girl.

My mom, Mary Theresa Garrity, was 46 when she died by suicide on January 19, 2003. As I write this, I am 44. I cannot believe that I am going to be older than she ever was in just a few short years. She had three children whom she loved immeasurably. She left behind my brother Adam (18), a senior in high school, and my brother Mike (14). To make matters worse, Mike became an orphan that day as his dad had died when he was seven. I was 27 and had been married to Darin for two years. I was the oldest child, the only "real" adult of my siblings, and I didn't really allow myself to grieve after she died. I had to do all of the business of her death, including taking guardianship of my brother Mike and selling her house. My husband and I focused on my brothers, and we did all we could to get them settled. It became an awful time of heartache and pain, and I rarely let my guard down. Of course, this backfired on me a few years later, when I had my first child. Only then did I feel the full loss of her death, and if not for the people in our lives, I am not sure how we would have survived those years. We allowed our community of friends and family to help us, love us, and take care of us through that season.

I imagine my mom must have struggled with depression and other mental health challenges in various ways her whole life. I certainly didn't know it as a child, but I am aware of it now. Her childhood was filled with many struggles, heartaches, traumas, and things I will never know about. What I do know is that her family loved her dearly, and close friends became like family. She also knew how to show love in a big way. My mom took so much pride in my brothers and me. She could not wait to be a grandma. She loved little children and had a special way with them, especially girls. She expressed her love through the language of "gifts." She would give you anything that you complimented her on in her home. To this day I still laugh at how she would say, "It's yours, I bought it for you," after telling her that you liked something.

She radiated joy to those that knew her; only her closest friends and family knew her pain. She worked very hard to heal. She wanted to believe that she could. She believed in therapy, and she learned to rely on a strong faith, although I truly think she never really believed that she "deserved" forgiveness or healing. She wanted medication to work for her. Unfortunately, she fell victim to years of alcohol abuse, so none of the medication trials were ever successful.

During her final year of life, she attempted suicide 15 times, which led to several hospitalization stays, including a 72-hour observation due to attempts and thoughts of suicide. The truth is, I became numb to the hospitalizations. Frustration and anger consumed me most of the time, so much so that her death actually surprised me. I thought it ironic—all the attempts—yet her death rocked me to the core as though I hadn't expected it. The guilt—oh, the guilt I felt! Survivor guilt after a suicide leaves no one unscathed.

My mom's legacy lives on. My daughter reminds me so much of her: the same fingers, love of life, etc. Actually, I remind myself of her, and I know the rest of our family would agree. Explaining death by suicide to my own little ones and trying to protect them from knowing the whole, awful truth was a large part of my fears as a parent. I couldn't find the "right time" to explain, it just came about when they were ready to understand. They have questions, so we talk honestly and openly about her life and her death. I still have questions, and I have regrets.

I am grateful for all the time I had with her, especially our last visit and our last phone conversation. So many of those phone conversations ended badly, but our last one did not. I hold on to that when the guilt starts to lie to me.

I know that she would be so proud of us and the life we created. My children love to hear stories about her, and they are getting to "know" her through those stories. We talk, share stories, and get together with friends and family who knew her. I believe it is the best way to honor her legacy. ~Dawn M.

Loss of a Father

Daddy was diagnosed with congestive heart failure in late 2008 after a triple bypass failed. His cardiologist allowed him to remain at home with me because he trusted me to record his vitals properly. I believe his cardiologist considered him a friend, as they had a physician-to-physician connection.

We created wonderful memories in the months that followed. It was my privilege to care for his daily needs. After a high fever developed and no option for dialysis, hospice became the next step. Daddy's heart was breaking and so was mine as we journeyed down this solemn path. I spent two weeks lodging in the hospital with him, always staying by his side. One afternoon, a friend took me to the cafeteria for a bit of a break. As I returned to his room, my brother met me in the hallway and said to hurry. A nurse listened for his heartbeat when I arrived at his room, but she could not find one. Daddy had slipped away while I was gone. I wasn't there for that final moment, and I sobbed as I held him. I could feel his body growing cold, and I just wanted to search for any trace of life, of warmth, of my father's love. Panic raced through me. I felt desperate and afraid to let him go. How was I to carry on without my hero? The man who had all the wisdom and compassion beyond words, humor and love, my go-to person who always had the right answer. It was April 16, 2009, the day life as I had always known it, ended. How would I ever survive without him?

Daddy's wake, funeral, and burial were very difficult; however, I was determined to honor this man who had contributed so much to my faith, joy, and understanding of life. He was a retired lieutenant in the US Navy, so they had a seven-gun salute and bagpipes playing "Amazing Grace" as they folded the flag that covered his casket. Warm tears rolled down my cheeks as they handed me the flag. It served as a perfect tribute to my father, my hero.

We shared many years of recovery in Alcoholics Anonymous together. Daddy died with 33 years of sobriety and I, at this time of writing, am approaching 40 years. He taught me what faith was; I honor him by holding on to it. ~Sally S.

Thank you, Daddy, and to quote you, it's only "goodbye for now." I love you and miss you every day. Your loving daughter, Sally

Loss of a Mother

For two weeks my sister and brother and I took turns staying by our mother's bedside in the hospital. I prayed for a miracle. I held her hand, talked to her, read scripture, and sang to her. I watched as she slept rather peacefully, all the while her body failing, and her breathing labored. I was 36 years old at the time. I felt so small, like I did as a child. I was afraid of losing her ... and then, she was gone. The miracle I prayed for never came... at least not the way I wanted. I remember at *that moment, when the quietness of her breathing had ended, looking into my sister's eyes. We silently searched for words, but only a steady stream of tears connected us. We were two grown women, clinging to one another, feeling like orphans. It seemed to me such an odd feeling, much like fear.*

Mothers selflessly give life, raise children to grow up and be independent. Then children are ready to move on, to strike out on their own, and maybe to start their own families, but few are ever ready to say their final goodbye. The void of grief exists, whether the memories are good or bad. I still miss my mom today as I did 25 years ago when her life was separated from mine. There are days I wish I could spend time with her or call her and say hello, talk about our lives, tell her all the details of the grandchildren that she never got a chance to meet. I wish I had realized when I was younger that you never outgrow your need for your mom... maybe I would have made more time and would have less regrets. ~Michelle K.

Loss of a Brother

My brother, Matt Reither, was killed suddenly on March 15, 1993, by a hit-and-run driver while pushing his disabled Jeep along I-94 near Eau Claire, WI. He was 21 years old. I was 19.

My world came crashing in on me, and I no longer wanted to be a part of it. Someone I loved was gone. I desperately wanted to see him, hug him, laugh with him, have a long conversation with him, and watch him play sports again. I just yearned to see him and hear his voice so the emptiness and the pain I felt in my heart would go away. Instead, every morning I would wake up in my college dorm room and feel the ache of his passing. I longed to be with him in heaven, and I wanted nothing to do with this world. In my grief, I thought, 'This world has only pain and suffering to offer me. God is going to do whatever He wants to do, so what's the point?' I thought I would just continue to exist on this earth, with this ache in my heart, until God called me home. Fortunately, I didn't stay in that mindset.

Five months later, my mom sent two of my siblings and me on a pilgrimage to Denver, Colorado. Pope John Paul II met with hundreds of thousands of young people from all over the world to pray and hear the Good News at that World Youth Day. The theme derived from John 10:10, where Jesus said, "I came that they might have life and have it abundantly" (ESV). JPII talked about a life centered on Christ, and he challenged us to live that kind of life and to "be not afraid." Everywhere I looked, there were people full of joy. I came back from that experience ready to not just exist, but to live.

I realized from that experience that every life mattered no matter how short or long it was, and if God wanted me to be on this earth, then I had a purpose and I was meant to live to the fullest. I also discovered that joy still exists in this world of suffering.

The pain of losing Matt has never gone away, but it has lessened, and I have learned through that pain that life is precious. I want to live every day to the fullest, knowing that joy and suffering are always a part of it. Although suffering is painful, working through it has led me to unimaginable joy. That joy comes from having hope and knowing that I will one day be reunited with Matt and all my loved ones that have passed since then. I will hear his voice and his laugh, and I will hug him again... someday. But until then, right here, right now, I have an abundant life to live. ~Loree N.

Loss of a Sister, a Brother-in-law, and a Niece

On January 7, 2017, a tragic car accident instantly took the life of my 14-year-old niece, followed two days later by the suicide loss of her father (my brother-in-law); ten days later, my sister died of complications from the accident, leaving only my 11-year-old niece who was in the car and witnessed the events.

The circumstances of our family tragedy were somewhat unique in that we were distracted from going through grief, staying busy with figuring out the ongoing care of my surviving niece. Grief, for me, did not start for months afterwards. I very purposefully set aside time to enter a season of brokenness. I went away for a week with my Bible, a journal, and a handful of books. I finally broke as I began to recognize just how removed I had been from the issues my sister had faced behind closed doors. How could I have been so unaware? Living a busy life, only one state away from my family, had gotten me to a place where I hardly knew my once closest friend, maid of honor, and baby sister—and now she was gone.

It is indescribable how God meets His children in that broken place. He ran to me and held me while continuing to whisper promises of blessing, hope, and comfort. I learned that loss is lonely! You can be surrounded with people who listen, but ultimately only God knows, hears, and understands. He is who I continue to go to when the pain of loss creeps back in. (Note: I recommend Ann Voskamp's book The Broken Way*).*

Being a person of action and control, I quickly recognized the things I could not control and accepted that God would use that which He allowed for His own good purposes. Eager to see those things come together, I was quick to say that God is in the recycling business and would use every piece of this somehow.

As time passed, with no apparent "connecting of the dots," God graciously gave me a clear message through a simple glass cube on a knickknack shelf near my front door. Thousands of dots inside the cube form the elegant design of a bull moose. I noticed for the first time that none of those dots were connected, but looking from the outside in, it appeared as a beautiful thing! In this life (represented by the cube), I continue to experience circumstances, both good and bad (represented by the etched dots), that make no sense, leaving me confused, flustered, and in awe. However, I believe God is excited to show me the masterpiece He is making of all the things in my beautiful, crazy life! ~Sarah H.

Loss through Miscarriage(s)

How do you make sense of a loss that you can't see or hold? I sometimes wonder if it would have been easier or harder to have held them, kissed them, and been able to say goodbyes. I would have had closure. But with so much undefined and unseen, and almost no evidence of my pain when most don't even know what I have gone through.... How, Lord, do I properly mourn (or bring others in to mourn with me) for someone I have never known other than in my dreams?

ADDITIONAL STORIES OF LOSS

Questions can be so overwhelming. There are so many that start as "questions" but lead to fear, doubt, blame, guilt, and depression to the point of questioning my faith. Not whether God is real or if I believe that His Word is true—I always believe—but things like this:

- *Would I be having all these questions if I truly trusted God?*
- *Do I still believe that God is a good Father?*
- *Can Jesus (with or without what I want) truly be enough for me?*
- *He is always enough, but can I find peace for myself that He is "enough" for me?*
- *Is it okay to even be having these crazy questions?*
- *Is it unbelief, sin, or a lack of faith that I'm struggling and hurting right now?*
- *Am I longing for something different than what I have been dealt?*

These are the kinds of thoughts that wreak more havoc on me than the dreadful pain I have suffered in the physical release and loss of babies. Sometimes the pain of miscarriage felt even worse than when I gave birth to the two children I now have. How grateful we are for the sons we are raising; they are a gift and a blessing to us. We endured the loss of thirteen pregnancies, with nine of those miscarriages between our two sons. Does having children to love and care for negate the pain of repeated loss—miscarriage after miscarriage? Does continuing to long for and to try to have more children negate the blessing of the children we have been given? Never!

Why don't I talk about it and share it? Because it is painful. But including others allows them to receive the blessings of learning, understanding, and coming alongside us. All this journey has stirred in me a determination to learn how to love well and to walk alongside others in whatever their own kind of pain might be. That is what I pray comes out of this, to the glory of our Almighty Healer and most Wonderful Counselor.

God is so good and so faithful! No matter what we walk through or the unsettled questions, His love is strong enough to sustain us and hold our soul at peace. We won't always get the answers we're searching for, but we can (maybe need) to still ourselves in deep search of Him. My experience changed me. It grew my heart, increased my compassion, my capacity to love, and my ability to empathize with others in the midst of their pain. I am better for all the "hard" and painful things I've walked through.

~Krista H.

Stillborn Loss

Our second son, Samuel John, was stillborn at 33 weeks of gestation in December of 2007. I had just turned 21. It was, and still is, the hardest thing I've ever endured. It happened so suddenly and with such finality. I felt like he hadn't been moving as much but didn't suspect the worst until we went to the hospital, and they spent 20 minutes trying to find his heartbeat. My doctor came in and told me, "I'm so sorry, but he's gone." My husband held me, and we cried together.

We had to wait an hour for the ultrasound tech to come and confirm his passing. They induced me then and gave me morphine, but it did nothing to help the pain I felt physically, mentally, and emotionally. We spent a day holding him, marveling at his perfect fingers and toes, his sweet nose and dark wispy hair. I vividly remember our departure from the hospital, riding down in the elevator, crying, and the nurse telling me she would take care of him. I honestly don't know how I wasn't screaming or hysterical. Leaving him behind on my bed was the most heart-wrenching thing I've ever had to do. Leaving the hospital with empty arms hurt so badly. The weeks and months that followed were dark. I thought I experienced chest pain, but it turned out to be anxiety. I didn't eat much or sleep well, and I lost weight. His death and funeral were right before Christmas.

Even now, years later, each year my heart is more tender, and I miss him especially at Christmas. Each new school year, I think of what grade he'd be in and wonder what his favorite things to do would be. Would he get along with his brothers? Would he have liked snuggling with me at bedtime like his brothers did?

It is a grief that will never go away. Time has helped the pain to be less sharp, but the sadness and ache is always there in the back of my mind. Just thinking about him for longer than 30 seconds makes me cry. The tears pour down my cheeks as I write this. Sometimes I feel like I failed him because I did not know that something went wrong. But I know that's not true ... I didn't know. I couldn't have known, and blaming myself is something that Satan wants. Our precious boy is safe and happy in heaven with Jesus, and we will see him again one day! I am so grateful for that hope and promise!

~Tessica T.

References / Resources

Songs for Healing

Need You Now (How Many Times) by Plumb

Worn by Tenth Avenue North

Exhale by Plumb

Thy Will by Hillary Scott & The Scott Family

I Am Not Alone by Kari Jobe

Come Alive (Dry Bones) by Lauren Daigle

Loyal by Lauren Daigle

Trust in You by Lauren Daigle

Tell Your Heart to Beat Again by Danny Gokey

I Can Only Imagine by Mercy Me

On the Wings of a Butterfly by Jimmy Scott

Goodbye's (The Saddest Word) by Celine Dion

Angel by Sarah McLachlan

Held by Natalie Grant

Your Hands by JJ Heller

You're Gonna Be Ok by Brian and Jenn Johnson

Blessings by Laura Story

The Hurt & The Healer by Mercy Me

In Jesus Name (God of Possible) by Katy Nichole

Books to Build and Restore

(With synopses by Bob Warnke)

The Bible; the Book of Job. This book opens with God's conversation with Satan and His permission for Satan to test Job. It describes Job's sudden loss, his secondary losses, and the counsel offered by his friends, as well as his faith and recovery. It closes with God's explanation of the loss and puts Job in his place when he questions God's grace.

The Blessings of Brokenness: Why God Allows Us to Go Through Hard Times. Charles F. Stanley. Zondervan Publishing House. ISBN# 0-310-20026-1. This book is a good parallel to the question of faith and "why did this happen to me" chapters in our life. (Personally, this was the sharpest and most soul-piercing of the books on loss. It discusses how God removes or attempts to remove the things/relationships in our lives that prevent God from being first.)

A Grace Disguised: How the Soul Grows Through Loss. (subtitle, expanded edition, 2005) Jerry L. Sittser. Zondervan Publishing House. ISBN:0-310-25895-2. First written in 1996 after a car accident that took Jerry's mother, wife, and daughter. Jerry is a college professor who teaches religious subjects, and this is a Christian-based look at why suffering is allowed and the grand plan of it all. This book is a must read for any type of loss or grieving condition.

Streams in the Desert. L.B. Cowman. Zondervan. 1997. ISBN: 978-0-310-21006-1. This is a daily devotional bringing comfort through scripture, poetry, and Cowman's personal experience of loss.

Silent Presence: A Companion Through the Journey of Grief. Mary O'Shaughnessy and Maureen Carey. Linus Publications. 2007. ISBN:1-934188-43-3. Written by a grief counselor who handled thousands of cases. This is divided into stages of grief and explains the normalcy of each stage. (Our grief group passed it around and we felt it was right on the mark with our varied stages.)

When Bad Things Happen to Good People. Harold S. Kushner. Schocken Books, NY. 2001. ISBN:0-8052-4193-0. This was originally written in 1981 and has been reprinted many times. It was one of the top-selling books in the "Spiritual" section of the bookstore. (It is not found in the Christian book section.) Written by a Jewish Rabbi from a large congregation in New York after losing his son. It has many suggestions on handling loss and relates Old Testament scriptures and his experiences in grief support. An interesting note on page 185 refers to being God's martyr or the devil's martyr.

One Minute After You Die. Erwin W. Lutzer. Moody Publishers, Chicago. 2015. ISBN: 978-0-8024-1411-3. This is concise and biblically based on the topic of heaven, how to get there ... or not. All explanations/claims reference numerous Scripture verses. Understandable and easy to read, broken into short chapters.

Answers to Your Questions about Heaven. David Jeremiah. Tyndale House Publishers. Carol Stream, Illinois. ISBN: 978-4964-0212—7 An easy read, laid out in chapters with a question and answer format. All answers are backed up by scripture references.

55 Answers to Questions About Life After Death. Mark Hitchcock. Multnomah Books. ISBN: 978-1-59052-436-7. This is laid out by topic and answers questions about death, heaven, hell, burial, cremation, salvation, etc. It is full of scripture backup and has extensive notes and references for further research.

Jesus the King: Understanding the Life and Death of the Son of God. Timothy Keller. Penguin Books Publishing. 2011. ISBN: 978-0-525-95210-7. Keller addresses questions like, "How can a loving God allow suffering?" He provides convincing reasons for his strong and unconditional belief in God.

Discernment. Henri J. M. Nouwen. Harper Collins Publishing. ISBN: 978-0-06-168616-0. This book helps us recognize the Holy Spirit promptings we often overlook—e.g., nature speaking to or uplifting us, people saying the right thing to acknowledge a direction, books we read, scripture we run across, etc.

The Wonderful Spirit-Filled Life. Charles F. Stanley. Thomas Nelson Publishing. ISBN: 0-7852-8693-4. An easy read, explaining the aspects of comfort, counsel, love, patience, and being neutral to the leading of the Holy Spirit.

It points out His leading through Scripture and using our conscience.

Why Suffering? Finding Meaning and Comfort When Life Doesn't Make Sense. Ravi Zacharias and Vince Vitale. Hachette Book Group. Pub. 10. 2014. ISBN: 978-1-4555-4971-9. This is an in-depth search into the purpose of suffering. The authors support biblical references with 10 philosophical reasons. Suffering is viewed from atheist, naturalist, Buddhist, and Islamic perspectives. It is written in a deep, contemplative manner, and may not be easy to catch everything on a first read-through. But after completing it, I believe it would be the best support of Christianity to someone questioning, "Is there even a loving God, and if so, why would a loving God allow suffering?"

Getting to the Other Side of Grief: Overcoming the Loss of a Spouse. Susan J. Zonnebelt-Smeenge, R.N., Ed.D. and Robert C. De Vries, D.Min., Ph.D. 1998. Baker Book Publishing. ISBN: 0-8010-5821-X. Co-authored by Susan, who lost her husband Rick, and Robert, who lost his wife Char. It is written from her perspective as a psychologist and his view as a pastor. It takes the reader through the phases of grief and healing, then into their new relationship, hurdles, and precautions.

The Purpose Driven Life. Rick Warren. 2002. Zondervan Press. Grand Rapids, Michigan. ISBN: 0-310-2057-9. This is a study that addresses life, loss, and our purpose for living, with reflection on what is important.

A Grief Observed. C. S. Lewis. 1961. Faber & Faber Ltd. London ISBN: 978-0-571-31087-6. A personal look into the journals written by C. S. Lewis after the loss of his wife. A powerful exploration of spiritual honesty.

Heaven. Randy Alcorn. 2004. Tyndale House ISBN-13: 978-0-8423-7942-7. Biblically based questions and answers about heaven.

Emily Lost Someone She Loved. Kathleen Fucci. 2015. Self-published Kathleen Fucci Ministries. ISBN-13: 978-0-9909-622-0-5. An illustrated children's story written from personal experience communicating the real emotions children feel when they lose someone they love. This book is a helpful resource for drawing out conversations with young children.

On Grief and Grieving: Finding the Meaning of Grief Through the Five Stages of Loss. Elisabeth Kübler-Ross, M.D. and David Kessler. 2005. Simon & Schuster, Inc. ISBN: 978-1-4767-7555-5. An in-depth expansion of the five stages of loss.

Finding Meaning: The Sixth Stage of Grief. David Kessler. 2019. Simon & Schuster, Inc. ISBN: 978-1-5011-9274-6. A faith-based book of stage five and beyond. Relative to read years after a loss.

Bible References

(With paraphrases by Bob Warnke)

Matthew 16:24 "Whoever wants to be my disciple must deny themselves and take up their cross and follow me." Taking up our cross can mean the current loss we carry.

John 11 This passage is about God's timing and how he used Lazarus' death. "If you (Jesus) had been here Lazarus would be alive" is applicable to our asking for healing during prayer. We think if He had listened to our prayer or was with us, our loved one would have lived. But what action, in John 11, best served God's purpose?

Psalm 68:5–6 "A father to the fatherless, a defender of widows, is God in his holy dwelling. God sets the lonely in families, he leads out the prisoners with singing; but the rebellious live in sun-scorched land." When our spirit is dry, it is like living in a sun-scorched land.

Psalm 22:11 "Do not be far from me, for trouble is near and there is no one to help." We should ask Him to walk with us, as He has the power to change our attitudes as well as those of the people around us.

Hebrews 2:14–15 "Since the children have flesh and blood, he too shared in their humanity so that by his death he might break the power of him who holds the power of death—that is, the devil—and free those who all their lives were held in slavery by their fear of death." As a believer we can overcome the fear of death.

Ecclesiastes 3:11 "He has made everything beautiful in its time. He has also set eternity in the human heart; yet no one can fathom what God has done from beginning to end." In our limited understanding, as we consider the reality of death, we can begin to receive life as a gift from God.

Jeremiah 1:5 "Before I formed you in the womb I knew you, before you were born I set you apart; I appointed you as a prophet to the nations." He knew us, and the deceased, and everyone who has ever lived, before we even took our first breath. He set us apart and appointed us to our positions.

Ephesians 2:10 "For we are God's handiwork, created in Christ Jesus to do good works, which God prepared in advance for us to do." Within the span of our lives, we each have a calling. Our existence is not random, and the deceased's existence was not random.

Verses by Topic

Questioning God—1 Peter 3:15 and 2 Peter 1:2, Ephesians 2:10, Romans 5, Jeremiah 20:11–13, Proverbs 2, Psalm 27

Confidence of heaven—Hebrews 2:14–15, Revelation 14:13, John 11:25-26; 2 Corinthians 5: 21, Romans 8:38–39, John 3:3

Recognizing death, the will of God, and suffering— Romans 5:12, Hebrews 2:4; 1 Peter 4:19; 1 Peter 5:10, Acts 2:23, Genesis 50:20, Isaiah 10:5–7; 2 Corinthians 2:4–5

*Beyond our understanding—*Romans 11:33, Deuteronomy 29:29; 1 Corinthians 2:9–10, Ephesians 1:9, Ephesians 3:4–5

*Conscience—*Romans 2:4

*New bodies—*2 Corinthians 5, Philippians 3:21, Revelation 21:4; 1 Corinthians 15:46–58

*Our existence is not random—*Jeremiah 1:4–5, Ephesians 2:10, Jeremiah 16:10

*God's grace—*2 Peter 1:2; 2 Corinthians 3:18, Jeremiah 20:11–13, Proverbs 2, Exodus 34:6

*God's love—*1 John 4:7, John 3:16

*Faith—*Hebrews 11

*A cry for understanding—*Psalm 27, Philippians 3, John 17:3

Definitions

Circumstance: A condition, fact, or event accompanying another or determining another. Synonyms: happening without intent or plan, an occurrence of importance of more than one frequency, setting up of the background.

Coincidence: A remarkable concurrence of events or circumstances without apparent causal connection.[4]

Conscience: The inner sense of what is right or wrong; the moral goodness of one's own conduct, intentions, or character with a feeling of obligation.[5] (Word search conscience in the Bible, and you find many scriptures on how the Holy Spirit relates to our conscience.)

Providence: The protective care of God as a spiritual power.[6] Example: They found their trust in His divine providence to be a source of comfort. Synonyms: God's will, divine intervention, predestination, predetermination, a life mapped out by providence.

Token: Something intended or supposed to represent or indicate another thing or an event, such as a sign or

---

[4] *Oxford English Dictionary*-Online. Definition of "Coincidence," accessed February 2025, https://www.oed.com/search/dictionary/?q=coincidence.

[5] *Merriam-Webster Dictionary*-Online. Definition of "Conscience," accessed February 2025, https://www.merriam-webster.com/dictionary/conscience.

[6] *Oxford English Dictionary*-Online. Definition of "Providence," accessed February 2025, https://www.oed.com/search/dictionary/?q=providence.

symbol. Example: The rainbow represented a token of God's covenant with Noah. Or a memorial of friendship; something by which the friendship of another person is to be kept in mind, a souvenir.

Triggers and Flashbacks: Also referred to as "episodic" memories, or in some instances, as PTSD (post-traumatic stress disorder). Also called ERPs (event-related potentials). Our brain is stimulated by recognizing triggers and sends a message to recall it from memory. (The claim: this occurs within 400 milliseconds after the stimulus.) Examples could be a smell, a taste, a view, a picture, an object, or an event that is like the past.

The Holy Spirit: When we recognize and believe the price that Christ paid for us (His sacrifice), the Spirit comes to live in us. The Spirit is there to guide us, using our conscience, if we are open to recognizing His presence. Examples: Romans 8, Galatians 3:1–6, and Galatians 5:16–26. There are many books on recognizing and utilizing the Holy Spirit (review the book resources).

Unhealthy Myths and Erroneous Beliefs of Grieving

(adapted from the book
Getting to the Other Side of Grief, pgs. 51–53)[7]

- Grieving extends over a set period of time. It moves through definable stages or phases, decreases after three months, and is completed after one year.
- The sudden death of a spouse is far worse than a prolonged illness. Anticipating loss makes it easier to accept.
- The loss of a child is worse than the loss of a spouse.
- You should keep yourself very busy to avoid thinking about your loss.
- Don't focus on the fact that your loved one has died. Don't talk about the loss, because when you don't think about it, your grief will pass faster.
- Happiness is gone forever after the death of a loved one.
- Wearing your wedding ring means you are grieving; if you remove it, you are done grieving and ready to date.
- You will never become a whole person again.

---

7 Susan J. Zonnebelt-Smeenge and Robert C. DeVries, *Getting to the Other Side of Grief: Overcoming the Loss of a Spouse.* (Grand Rapids, MI: Baker Books, 1998), 51–53.

- Going places by yourself means you are undesirable, inferior, or inadequate.
- Having fun or laughing while in the grieving process means you did not really love the person who died.
- After the loved one has passed, you must continue on with the wishes they expressed when alive.
- Having friends of the opposite sex when widowed must mean you are looking for a dating or romantic relationship.
- Being alone is lonely, and living by yourself is less desirable than with a partner.
- If you had a happy and loving relationship prior to your spouse's death, it is unlikely a new partner can measure up to prior experience.
- Men more so than women need to have better self-control and handle grief cognitively (i.e., master their emotions, not cry, etc.).

Notes

Keller, Timothy. *Jesus the King: Understanding the Life and Death of the Son of God.* 2011. Penguin Books Publishing: New York, NY.

Kübler-Ross, Elisabeth. *On Death and Dying.* 1969. Scribner: New York, NY.

Merriam-Webster Dictionary-Online. Definition of "Conscience," accessed February 2025, https://www.merriam-webster.com/dictionary/conscience.

O'Shaughnessy, Mary and Maureen Carey. *Silent Presence: A Companion Through the Journey of Grief.* 2007. Linus Publications: Deer Park, NY.

Oxford English Dictionary. Definition of "Coincidence," accessed February 2025, https://www.oed.com/search/dictionary/?q=coincidence.

Oxford English Dictionary. Definition of "Providence," accessed February 2025, https://www.oed.com/search/dictionary/?q=providence.

Zonnebelt-Smeenge, Susan J. and Robert C. De Vries. *Getting to the Other Side of Grief: Overcoming the Loss of a Spouse.* 1998. Baker Books: Grand Rapids, MI.

Journaling

Suggestions and prompts: Journaling can be used to track progress, identify when you are stuck, and/or record present-time emotions.

Write about your loved one...

- Their strengths, personality, hobbies, passions, hopes and dreams, etc.
- Name three memories you don't want to lose.
- What do you do, or plan to do, to keep their memory alive?
- If you knew the end was coming prior to their passing, what did you do to prepare them, yourself, or your family?
- If this was a sudden death, what do you wish you had done weeks, months, or years prior?
- Do you have any regrets that could now be turned into action items (to support or prevent someone else from a difficulty)?
- What do you wish you had asked or said prior to their death?

- What did you value most about your relationship?
- Do you need to ask them or yourself for forgiveness?
- List the promises you and the deceased made while living. Then answer if you will follow through after their death. Why or why not?
- Identify the values you shared together that you will not deviate from.
- What do you want to change in your life now? Do you have prayers for the future?
- Describe yourself from the point of view of the deceased. What can you do to build upon that foundation?
- Journal about positive ways you can approach special dates or holidays.

My Story

A Closing Note

We hope you have found this study guide to be a comfort during this difficult season of life. This support material has been written as a not-for-profit compilation to help others along their journey of loss. If you found this helpful, then we would ask that you prayerfully consider starting a grief group to help others.

The purpose of a grief group is to come alongside those that are grieving the death of a loved one. Compassion, patience, and faith are the key ingredients.

As a facilitator, you are not expected to fix anyone or to have all the answers. Simply extend God's grace and love to each one present and allow time for healing. From our experience, the formation of a cohesive group depends on the comfort level of the members. They should understand they are not alone in their journey and feel safe enough to share their experiences in a confidential setting.

If you are interested in learning more about starting a grief group in your area and receiving a facilitator's instructional packet, please email us at: graceforthegrieving@gmail.com.

May God bless you as you continue to heal.

Jeannine, Bob, Maureen, John, Harriet, Burt, Jill, and Karen

About the Contributors...

Jeannine Richardson   Bob Warnke   Maureen Revak   John Kidder

Harriet Perry   Burt Groenheim   Jill Groenheim   Karen Huebschman

The contributors of Grace for the Grieving all live in small neighboring communities in northwestern Wisconsin. Their journey together began in 2016 at a local grief group. They started as acquaintances and strangers, brought together by the common thread of loss. In sharing their experiences with one another they found that hope, healing, and new friendships began. This is a compilation of their personal stories and practical application for navigating through the emotional ebb and flow that comes from losing someone you love. Their encouragement to the bereaved is gently woven through its pages.

To learn more about their individual stories, see the "Our Stories" section at the beginning of the book.

Made in the USA
Monee, IL
02 July 2025